Spirit of Change

Voices of Hope

In this remarkable collection former Buddhist monk Christopher Titmuss interviews people who are working for change around the world, including a psychotherapist who became committed to the cause of human rights after a visit to Nicaragua and an Italian housewife whose spirituality blossoms even as her body is dying of cancer. The men and women interviewed address such pressing issues as:

- bridging social, cultural, and religious differences

- finding individual peace and working for global peace and disarmament

- empowering women to liberate themselves from society's limiting roles and structures

- overcoming our society's obsession with material things

- protecting and saving the environment

The interviews in this book are portraits of enlightenment, offering pathways for spiritual awakening and ideas for making radical changes in our lives and our world.

About the Author

Christopher Titmuss, 46, was an international news reporter working in London, Istanbul, Laos, and Australia. In 1970 he was ordained a Buddhist monk, and spent six years in Thailand and India. He now teaches engaged spirituality and insight meditation around the world.

He is the co-founder of various spiritual communities and centers, including Gaia House, an intensive meditation center in Denbury, Devon, England and the Sharpham North Community, Ashprington, Totnes, Devon.

Christopher is a member and supporter of a number of organizations working for people and planet. He is on the international board of the Buddhist Peace Fellowship. In the June 1987 general election in Britain, he stood for parliament as the Green Party candidate for the constituency of Totnes, where he lives with his daughter, Nshorna.

Spirit *of* Change

Voices of Hope for a Better World

Christopher Titmuss

Library of Congress Cataloging-in-Publication Data

Titmuss, Christopher
Spirit of change : voices of hope for a better world /
by Christopher Titmuss.
p. cm.
ISBN 0-89793-104-1 : $19.95 — ISBN 0-89793-094-0 : $9.95
1. Social problems—Moral and ethical aspects. 2. Life.
3. Conduct of life. 4. Human ecology—Moral and ethical aspects.
I. Title
HN18.T55 1992
361.1—dc20   92-2853
CIP

Cover Design: Paula Schlosser Design   Book design: *Qalagraphia*
Project Editor: Lisa E. Lee   Editor: Jackie Melvin
Production Manager: Paul J. Frindt
Marketing: Corrine M. Sahli   Promotion: Robin Donovan
Customer Service: Victor Campbell
Publisher: Kiran S. Rana

Set in Adobe Garamond by 847 Communications, Alameda, CA
Printed and bound by Patterson Printing, Benton Harbor, MI
Manufactured in the United States of America

9 8 7 6 5 4 3 2 1   First edition

Contents

Acknowledgements

Between 1984 and 1990 I traveled in Australia, Continental Europe, England, India, Thailand, and the United States conducting interviews with people concerned with engaged spirituality, inner life, the current psychological and spiritual climate, and our relationship to the world. Selections of these interviews were originally published in two volumes in England as *Spirit for Change* and *Freedom of the Spirit*.

To all the people I interviewed, who kindly found time in their full schedules to meet with me, I express heartfelt thanks. Each one communicated a spiritual awareness and understanding of the issues directly affecting all our lives and the planet.

I wish to express my appreciation to Henrietta Rogell who has worked continuously with me on the typescript.

Heartfelt thanks also go to Gwanwyn Williams, who kindly gave much assistance in transcribing many of the tapes, as well as to Evelyn Sweeney, Rose Deiss, and Walter Schwarz. Also special thanks to Gill Farrar-Halls for her editing skills.

I also wish to thank various friends who set up several of the interviews for me, including David Arnot, James Baraz, Catherine Ingram, Phra Achaan Dhammadaro, Stephan and Martine Batchelor, Christine Engels, Jim Fowler, Corrado Pensa, Francesca Rusciani, and Bhikkhu Pannavudho.

I wish to express appreciation to Jon Carpenter of Green Print who has given continuous support to the publication of two volumes of these interviews.

May all people, creatures, and the planet
live in peace and harmony

A Personal Preface

No doubt some of us can remember a turning point, a moment in which a sense of the interconnectedness between the planet and ourselves was awakened. For me, this fusion of personal and global awareness took place on a flight to Boston in the summer of 1980.

I was sitting in a window seat aimlessly staring out of the window into the summer sky and the ocean below. Without preparation or thought, two mental wires suddenly fused. One was the spiritual element, in which I had a sustained and abiding interest. The other was the area of political action, which had been dormant in me for a decade. What struck me on this otherwise forgettable flight was that spiritual awareness, self-knowledge, meditation, psychotherapy, religious beliefs, and experiences are potentially the raw material for political awareness and service.

One of the features of the nonviolent movement toward social and global change is the noticeable lack of leaders. Today we are moving away, thankfully, from the charismatic and visionary individual toward small collectives specializing in particular fields for the health, welfare, and liberation of the planet from its pain.

Social and psychological forces cannot be separated from each other. There are those who claim that social forces condition the mind into forms of behavior. This view suggests that we have to change society, we have to campaign against the dictatorship of the marketplace and state control. In this view, society's obsession with producing and consuming sweeps all along in its wake—like the creatures in the biblical story who blindly rush over the edge of the cliff.

Others uphold the view that people have to change themselves first. This is a continuation of the philosophy of individualism. Since the core idea lies within each individual, then each person has to work on themselves, they claim. Each person has to work out their own fear. Only when people are willing to look into their own lives and see into their conditioned mind can there be real hope of stopping humanity from running headlong over the edge.

Perhaps both views—of individualism and of society as a collective—are extremes. Concentration on either hinders us from understanding that psychological and social forces are not separate from each other. If we work to change society but neglect our own way of living, we are hypocrites. If we are merely engaged in various forms of navel-gazing—cherishing religious beliefs, doing body work, meditation, psychotherapy, guru devotion—we subscribe to a personal salvation alienated from the totality of life.

We have the responsibility to examine the quality of our inner and personal lives. We also need to be aware of the way social, economic, and political forces impact on our consciousness. I believe we need to explore the wide variety of resources available for both inner and outer change. Surely only the naive and the dogmatic will claim that the solution to personal and global issues resides exclusively with a particular person or book or religious, scientific, or political viewpoint.

This book is a series of interviews with women and men on themes of engaged spirituality.

What is communicated by each is the willingness to take risks, to raise difficult questions about the accepted way of things, and to explore the potential for change through words and actions. There is a twofold intention behind this book. First, it provides us with some direct insights into ourselves and the world we live in. Second, it may serve as a inspiration to engage in that noble human activity of exploration into the nature of things and service to others.

This collection of interviews is primarily an examination

of the significance of our inner life in relationship to social and global realities. The people interviewed in this book are not high priests or priestesses of their particular fields. They are not people we need project our hopes on to. Rather, they are voices of concern, articulate voices who communicate what might be described as a global psychology. I have spoken to them about their commitments. Several of them have participated in retreats on engaged spirituality with me. Some of them are friends.

I would also like this book to be read by future generations so they will know that in this enduring time of serious human and global problems there *were* voices of concern—and there was a spirit of change.

Christopher Titmuss
Totnes, Devon, England

A Reduction of Our Needs

An interview with Satish Kumar

During the 1960s, Satish Kumar and a companion made a two-and-a-half-year walk for peace from his home country of India through Pakistan, Afghanistan, Iran, the Soviet Union, Poland, East and West Germany, Belgium, France, England, and America. They carried no money on this 8,000-mile walk, depending totally on the hospitality and goodwill of the people of each country. The story of this marathon walk is told in his book, *No Destination*. Satish was offered an award from the Soviet Union for the book but declined it, saying that Russia must first release its imprisoned dissident writers.

Satish entered into the religious life as a nine year old, when he became a Jain monk. The Jain religion calls for total dedication to respecting all sentient life and protecting it from pain. By the time he was eighteen years old, he had decided to combine spiritual practices with social action. He left the monkhood and joined the Gandhian movement under Vinoba Bhave. Satish joined Vinoba in persuading landlords to donate land to the landless—the aim of which was to establish a peaceful economic revolution. Vinoba later encouraged Satish and his friend to make the long walk for peace.

In 1968, Satish was invited to England by Christian Aid to establish and direct the London School of Nonviolence. He taught courses in nonviolent action, sustainable economics, and development in the Third World. During this period he became a close friend of E.F. Schumacher, a founding father of the Green movement and author of the classic Green economics, *Small Is Beautiful*.

In the early 1970s, Satish was invited to become editor of

Resurgence, a thoughtful and influential journal of Green economics and politics, ecology, and holistic awareness. After the death of E.F. Schumacher in 1977, he founded the Schumacher Society in honor of the economist. He has been president of the society since its foundation and organizes and presides over the internationally respected Schumacher Memorial Lectures held in Britain every autumn.

Satish believes that it is the responsibility of the state to fund education and that the responsibility for curriculum and management rests with the school administrators, teachers, parents, and children. In 1982, Satish founded the Small School in Hartland, North Devon, with nine children, to follow through with his ideology. The enrollment has now increased to more than thirty children.

The latest project that Satish has instigated is the establishment of a publishing house, called Green Books, specializing in Green and global issues.

Satish lives in Hartland with his wife and two children. The interview was conducted at the Sharpham community.

•

SK: I was born into a very orthodox Jain family. My mother was a very, very devout Jain, and what I learned about the Jain religion was mainly from her. The most important thing I realized, which is even more clear now, was that my mother saw everything in the world—whether a plant, a tree, a bird, a piece of grass, a rock, or human being—as having a spirit. And therefore she practiced a complete and utter nonviolence to all beings, living and not living.

CT: Her perception that everything has a spirit or soul brought forth a great reverence for life.

SK: Reverence. That's the word. She thought that as human beings we have to practice reduction of our needs, a reduction of dependence on other things and other beings. Therefore, for example, we practiced complete vegetarianism. A Jain on no account will kill an animal to eat. That is a reduction of need. My mother made a list of fifty items, including rice, mangoes, cauliflower, lentils, and certain spices, and said, "Among all the vegetarian foods, I will eat only these fifty items." So her needs were reduced. When it came to travel, she would not go in any direction that she wanted. She would say, "I will only travel twenty miles today, only in the eastern direction, going and coming back." She would not go off somewhere on the spur of the moment wherever she liked because even when you are traveling you are taking space, you are using the earth, you are treading on the grass and harming beings, living or not living. Therefore she would reduce her travel needs. With clothing she would say, "I need only twenty items of clothing." At no time would she have more than twenty items. The moment she bought one new item of clothing, she would have to make sure that one piece of clothing was old enough to give away or to use as rags. So we can reduce our needs by observing how many possessions we have. The most fundamental principles of Jain religion are nonpossession and nonviolence.

CT: You had this influence right from conception. In your own way, you took it a step further by becoming a monk

SK: That's right. When I was nine years old, I came in close contact with the monks because my mother was always going to meet with them. The monks said, "If you are living in the world with a family, a business, a house, however much care you take, you can never practice nonviolence and nonpossession to its utmost limits. Only by becoming a monk and renouncing all possessions and all forms of violence, as well as renouncing family and home, can you really set an example of complete and total nonviolence and nonpossession." And that idea attracted me very much. I thought at least some people are practicing an extreme form of nonviolence and nonattachment; not a middle path, but an extreme path. It would be a good thing to show the world how little one really needs. That really attracted me very much, even though I was only nine.

And that is where I believe that something must have come to me from my previous life, that at the age of nine I could have such a determined and passionate thought to become a monk in such an extreme form.

CT: You made a very long journey by foot from India to the West. What was the impact of the West upon you?

SK: In the beginning, when I first came to the West, it was a cultural shock for me. When I saw people were acquiring things they didn't really need, I was shocked. At heart, I was a monk, though at this time I had left the outer form of the monastic life. I felt this kind of acquisitive and materialistic culture of the West was having an influence and impact on the whole world. And perhaps it was useful for me to talk to and live with people in the West while practicing some of the principles of nonpossession and nonviolence, such as being vegetarian, not having the usual possessions of life like a television or car, which people take for granted as a normal part of living. They always ask me, how can you live in the countryside in such a remote place and not have a car? How do you manage? How do you move about? And I say that I walk wherever I need to walk. I have two legs. People have forgotten that they have two legs and these legs can take you anywhere.

CT: How did you become exposed to Fritz Schumacher's teachings and the Green philosophy?

SK: When I came to live in the West, because of the cultural shock I started to look around for kindred spirits. I looked for people who had some spiritual, ecological values which were in keeping with my Jain training and background. During that time I came across an article by E.F. Schumacher called "Buddhist Economics." In essence, Jain economics and Buddhist economics are very similar. Immediately being gripped and enchanted by what I read, I wrote to Schumacher. I was very happy to receive his response and we set up a meeting. Immediately we got on very well together. From the first meeting in 1968 we became such good friends that we thought we had known each other for a long time, even though we had not met before. From then until the time that he died we remained very close.

Schumacher was closely associated with *Resurgence* magazine and it was through him and the former editor, John Papworth, that I came to be editor. They said I was a Gandhian and a Jain, and Schumacher said, "The Jain religion must be one of the most ecological religions in the world. Therefore if you bring those values and combine them with the conservation and the ecological movement of the West, that will be a very useful thing to do."

> "You can find the key to Schumacher's thinking in three sentences. Number one is—keep it small. Number two is—keep it simple. Number three is—keep it nonviolent."

CT: You had years of contact with Schumacher, who is regarded as a founding father of the Green movement. How would you describe his major themes?

SK: You can find the key to Schumacher's thinking in three sentences. Number one is—keep it small. Number two is—keep it simple. Number three is—keep it nonviolent. Whether it is a technology, a social or political organization, or economics that you're dealing with, you keep it small on a human scale so that the intimacy of human relationship is never destroyed. Bigness always undermines the human scale and human relationship. The moment you grow too big you have to follow a certain set of rules to work things out.

CT: Then those of us in the Green movement are in a paradox. Schumacher and others say, "Keep it small," and we are also saying we want the Green movement to grow.

SK: If you keep it small, simple, and nonviolent, there is still room for growth, but in quality, not just in quantity. Our scientific and technological work is always looking for quantitative growth which can be measured. Schumacher says that you can grow inwardly; you can improve the quality in your relationship, in your homes, villages, farms, and factories, and thus find a happier environment with a more wholesome lifestyle. And that's the growth which he talked about. He didn't talk about growing in numbers. He was talking about growing in the quality of life.

CT: You have lived a life of simplicity, severity, and austerity in India. Now you live in the West and all that goes with that. Have you wondered whether there has been some compromise of values?

SK: I don't think there has been a compromise. I think that by going through the rigorous discipline of a Jain monk I have learned to be inwardly detached. Once you have learned that stage of being, then you can get in the midst of the hubble-bubble of the world and still be detached. I have learned that way and I feel quite detached and not overwhelmed by possessions nor in any way oppressed by the Western world.

CT: In this detached attitude toward possessions, is it your view that possessions only have utilitarian value?

SK: I would say possessions not only have a utilitarian value, possessions are transformed as objects of relationship, and, therefore, even those objects become your companions and friends. Like this sweater I'm wearing. It is not a utilitarian sweater but it is a sweater with which I have a friendship and a relationship. The sweater is protecting me and I am protecting the sweater. I am looking after the sweater, washing it, cleaning it, and keeping it neat and tidy so that in ten years' time I might be wearing the same sweater. I am looking after it as a friend. In return the sweater is being very compassionate and very kind to me. It is protecting me from the rain, and from the cold, and so on. So the possessions I have are few. I have them not as utilitarian objects but as friends.

In the same way, if I am in a home, it is God's home—it is a sacred home, a holy place. It is the home where I can sit down. I can meditate. I can have guests. I can offer hospitality. I can look after my children. I can let them grow there. I can love my family. So a home is a spiritual place and not a matter of status or of possession or investment. I don't possess such thought at all. I have no interest in its monetary value. My interest is in its spiritual value. If we can transform our attitude in that way, then everything that we use to make our home, all the materials of the earth—slates, stones, wood, fiber, etc.—contribute to making home life rich, spiritual, and sacred.

CT: You had the gift of a mother deeply committed to ecological values. You had the discipline and training of the Jain monkhood. Most of us have neither, therefore our models have been different.

SK: People who are concerned with such matters as you express have to find kindred spirits. One, two, ten, no matter how many, because kindred spirits can give mutual support and mutual nourishment to each other. In the Jain and Buddhist tradition, this is called *sangha*—people giving nourishment to each other. So I would say that people who are seeking something different, which is spiritual, sacred, fundamental, and in harmony with themselves, their work, and nature, have to seek out people who are supportive to that approach and not live surrounded by people who are always encouraging them to buy more, possess more, go faster, become successful, gain richness and fame. If you haven't got the discipline of a Jain or Buddhist, or a background like I had with my mother, at least now you can find kindred spirits. They are certainly around. Perhaps you can find companionship in your neighborhood, so you are supported and so you are not living in the desert of materialism.

CT: Would you say that in the last fifteen years the "desert of materialism" has been more deeply questioned?

SK: Yes, I see that. When I came fifteen years ago to Britain, if you went around looking for a vegetarian restaurant, you would have to search hard to find five or ten in the whole country. Now in almost every town you can find one. You can say the same thing about wholefoods. When I came, food was mass-produced and mostly canned. People wanted fast food and junk food. They were just not interested in wholesome food. What they ate was not really their concern. It was much more a matter of convenience. Now people are concerned with what they eat, the kind of food, and how it is grown. So wholefood shops have sprung up.

Fifteen years ago the word "meditation" was a weird word. Now we can learn to meditate and be part of a normal society. So the consciousness has changed. These are examples that show that something is going on. Something is happening. Even though the governments and financial institutions, the multinational corporations, the schools and hospitals have not changed, the individual people within them are questioning.

CT: These questions are being asked, yet there seems to be very little inroad in terms of Buddhist economics. The emphasis of the present Western governments, which influences the teachers of economics in our schools, is to stress a wealth-creating society.

SK: I agree with you. Government thinking and policy has not changes, but on the grassroots level I think there are many more Buddhist economics-oriented projects and businesses now than there were fifteen years ago. In the last census in Britain, the population of the big cities is decreasing and the rural areas increasing. Devon has increased by six percent and Norfolk and Suffolk by nine percent. The population of the larger cities of Birmingham, Manchester, London, and Glasgow is decreasing. The trend has changed, and the trend is toward going back to the countryside, starting a small business, a craft shop or a wholefood shop, entering into a livelihood which is more in harmony with yourself and your ideals. And those things are growing. It is my hope that in the next five to ten years un-employed people will find some self-employment which is useful, ecologically sound, and spiritually rewarding. I think the problem is not unemployment. The problem is employment. People must have the chance to find good work.

CT: You are speaking about the *form* of employment?

SK: People are working in nuclear power stations; people are working in factories where they are mass-producing cars, armaments, clothing, tele- visions, and newspapers. All these kinds of jobs are essentially soul-destroying, spirit-destroying, nature-destroying, world-destroying, and planet-destroying.

The thing is that all civilizations come, rise, and fall. The Roman empire, the Egyptian empire, the British empire, all have come and gone. Now we are going through the industrial empire, where technology, science, rationalism, and analytical thinking are dominant. As a result, our arts, our work, our mode of production, our culture has been affected by industrial, mechanistic growth. This will come to an end, as every civilization has to come to an end, since the world is impermanent and changing and nothing can last forever.

We are not going back, but we are transforming the present structure to be much more human. People call "transformation" going back. Going back to what? Going back to the first principle of love and compassion in mutual help and support. And these values can create more harmonious modes of work and production and more creativity in the arts. We have to talk in terms of transformation rather than returning to a primitive or preindustrial society.

CT: You and your family have spent recent years in a remote North Devon village. What have you been doing there?

SK: I have been living. [He smiles.] I think that I can do nothing more important than to love, to be. But outwardly people see how I live, namely I edit the magazine *Resurgence*, because I think it is very important that we don't live with our ideas in isolation. We are not isolated beings; we are part of this network of society. Communicating with society is one of the major concerns that I have. Through *Resurgence* I have been able to offer a forum and a platform, a medium of communication, so that people can see a different way of living, of thinking, of working. So *Resurgence* has been my main work, but I don't do it as a job or profession; I do it as a service to society, a communication with society.

I see it in a context with the rest of my living: with my family, working on the land, growing food, looking after the cow, and being a little bit self-sufficient. This context is very important to me. If you see my life, one third is devoted to my intellectual work on *Resurgence*. The second third is devoted to my physical activities, like working in the garden, milking the cow, cooking the food, cleaning the house. The remaining third is devoted to the emotional sphere: my relationship with my children, wife, and friends, with my guests, when receiving people or staying with others. Throughout these three spheres there is a thread which you cannot see. You can see the beads, but you cannot see the thread. The thread is spiritual. So my intellectual work, my physical work, and my emotional work are in the service of the spirit.

> "I think it is very important that we don't live with our ideas in isolation. We are not isolated beings; we are part of this network of society."

CT: What does the word "spiritual" mean for you?

SK: To me, spiritual means something which is more than meets the eye. For example, I talked about my sweater and my relationship with it. That relationship is something that you cannot see outwardly, it is my inner spiritual understanding and awareness, and this I am trying to develop all the time through meditation, study, and through communication. It also involves the question of service. It touches upon my relationship with my wife, June, with my children and neighbors, and with people who are in need. Now what is the inspiration for that service? What is the inspiration of working in the garden? The inspiration is spiritual. So all of my activities have to stem from that basis.

This spiritual approach to life, which is so subtle, which cannot be described in worlds or be analyzed or really even be spoken about, but can be felt, is where you can find a sense of fulfillment, the meaning of life can only be fulfilled through this spiritual awareness. For a human being who does not feel fulfilled, the first thing is to stop wherever you are. If you are not happy with your life, your work, with the way you are, and you don't really know where you are going and you feel lost, you stop. There is no point in continuing to go. Then you will meet some passersby. When you do, ask them the way. Somebody will help. There will be those who will say, "I don't know," and those who'll say, "Don't bother me." After asking with real inquiry, somebody you meet will know where you want to go. And yet, you have to find your own way, not follow where somebody else is going to go, where somebody else wants you to go. We all have our destiny and our path. But there are people who will help you to find your way, and they are the people I call kindred spirits.

CT: We may say that the path itself, when deeply comprehended, is so fulfilling that there is no destination.

SK: Yes. Yes. There is no destination. Life is here and all the time we are moving without a destination.

The Awakening of Women

An interview with Christina Feldman

I first met Christina Feldman in 1974, in Dharamsala, India, in the foothills of the Himalayas. She was twenty-two years old, married, and engaged full time in the study and practice of Mahayana Buddhism. Her spiritual journey took her to India from Canada when she was seventeen years old.

As she recalls, she found herself looking first to authority and tradition for the answers she was seeking. Living in Dharamsala she was exposed to the Tibetan teachings and was one of the first students of the respected teacher Geshe Rabten. She also participated in a number of intensive meditation retreats with teachers, including myself, who were influenced by the Theravada Buddhist tradition.

In 1975, I lived in Dalhousie for five months, conducting retreats in some large old rented houses in that part of the Himalayan foothills. Some sixty people participated in the program, including Christina. Not many weeks went by before we began to recognize that Christina had much to offer in the way of insight and understanding of the human condition.

Since that time she has facilitated retreats throughout the world, sometimes working with other teachers, including myself. Her quiet, unblemished, matter-of-fact talks are given to groups of people from all walks of life. More than one hundred of her talks are on tape.

Born in Yorkshire, she spent the first five years of her life in England, until her parents emigrated to Canada. She returned to live in England in May 1977. In September of that year, Christina and I cofounded the Gilletts Community in Smarden, Kent, where twenty us lived in an eleven-bedroom house.

Now married to Mick Rusling, a social worker, she has two children, Sara and Aaron. In 1983 she moved from Gilletts to Totnes, Devon, where she cofounded Gaia House, an international retreat center. She is also a member of the international board of the Buddhist Peace Fellowship. In recent years, Christina has expanded the form of her retreats to include separate groups for families and for women.

Christina says that we have to be willing to risk the loss of external dependency, affirmation, and approval if we are to know ourselves deeply. The "validity of our spirituality can only be qualified by our own experience and understanding. Through meditation, we can untangle the conditioning that leads us to prostrate ourselves before authority." Christina continues to make it clear that she does not want to be perceived as an authority, in any area.

Her book, *Woman Awake,* is an inquiry into and a celebration of women's spirituality. Recently she coauthored *Stories of the Spirit, Stories of the Heart* with Jack Kornfield. Our interview explores women's issues today.

•

CT: At the present time, we are experiencing a noticeable and significant change in the consciousness of women as they discover in fresh ways the sense of their authority. How can a woman guard against imitating some of the ways in which men have used and abused power?

CF: As women become increasingly conscious of themselves, they become correspondingly aware of the dynamic of power. Women also see the negative conditioning they carry. Part of women's conditioning is to believe that the real power centers exist primarily outside of themselves. These outside power centers have the authority to dispense values, models, and rules that govern our appearance, presentation, direction, and goals. These centers also dispense approval and disapproval, acceptability and unacceptability. Part of most women's conditioning is to believe these powers are somewhat infallible.

The destructive effect of this is that women begin pursuing models of how they think they should be in order to be acceptable, feel worthy, and appear feminine. To follow that way of living is basically a way of disempowering ourselves, because there is a constant looking for credentials to see whether we have succeeded or failed in conforming to these models.

CT: So the negative conditioning for a woman is to place authority and power outside of herself.

CF: Yes, the final arbiter of worthiness is placed in anything that's perceived to have authority—institutions, social values, traditions, or beliefs. Anything can seem to have the power to dispense acceptability.

CT: Are women choosing to place this power outwardly?

CF: It's not a conscious choice. It is a collusion between women and those who are either set up or set themselves up as authorities. It's an unconscious choice. It is rooted in not knowing any source of inner empowerment. Women don't necessarily acknowledge this as long as they are alienated from a source of inner empowerment.

Also, these power centers exist only as long as they are believed in. For example, the church may say women cannot become priests. If that power center is not believed in, then those dictates fall in a vacuum. Buddhist monks may say that women can't have equal ordination. If that power isn't given to the monks, then the dictate doesn't have any meaning.

CT: A woman may say, "Yes, I keep transferring this power to these voices of authority. I can't stop myself from doing it. I just don't seem to believe in myself, in my gender. What can I do?" What would you say?

CF: The first step is to be really conscious that she is actually doing that, that she is actually giving her power away. The first step of being conscious is also the first step in bringing about change. What follows from that is to find support for such a change so there comes about the courage to question how infallible these power centers are.

CT: How would you define "power" in this context?

CF: I define power as an energy that holds the capacity to transform or change. It is neither negative nor positive. It is an energy that everyone has within themselves. What we are primarily exposed to in our life is a degeneration of power. Negative power is frequently backed by motives of fear and insecurity and the taking up of fixed positions.

Often, within institutions, the powers that be are very unwilling to change. They don't wish to give up their power base at all or their role in that power base. If it is unacceptable, a woman has to step out of it. In one sense, to resist a negative power structure gives as much power to it as to subscribe to it. The power structure still supports the belief that it exists as a power center and is worthy of obedience or resistance. I am saying this on the basis that the particular institution in question is unwilling to change. Power centers have, of course, an investment in being a power center. This investment is propped up by unfathomable depths of insecurity and fear. So any changes will initially bring about a lot of resistance.

> "It's important for women to look for radically new sources of power and new ways of using power. Otherwise women will begin to operate power centers in the same way—supported basically by fear and insecurity."

CT: What else is important to bring about change?

CF: It's important for women to look for radically new sources of power and new ways of using power. Otherwise women will begin to operate power centers in the same way—supported basically by fear and insecurity. This means that no real change has taken place. If women can discover sources of power within themselves, a pure power, then the power will be rooted in wisdom, rooted in inner trust. This power is not caught up in a struggle between for and against, or a struggle to convert or manipulate. Women who are rooted in trust and wisdom will simply be saying that this is what we understand to be true.

CT: And if there is still an unwillingness to be heard?

CF: Then the ingredients for change are simply not there. One way that women can offer change is by using power in a qualitatively different way—by offering clear alternatives.

CT: But isn't sustained resistance to the status quo a valid activity?

CF: Yes, it is. For example, I find myself rubbing up against traditional Buddhists. I know that Theravada Buddhism [one of the main Buddhist traditions] isn't going to change overnight, if at all, in its attitude towards women's ordination. The rules don't allow it. I don't say, "Well, forget it. I'm not going to deal with you guys." I am going to go on speaking the truth as I see it. I hope somewhere it will touch someone and encourage them to question. That doesn't mean to say I wouldn't explore a viable alternative. I don't feel bound to the inequalities the tradition may uphold, therefore I can draw upon the richness of the tradition without in any way being limited by it.

CT: What sort of things do you have in mind when you say "viable alternatives?"

CF: For example, participating in women's retreats. Women's retreats create an environment in which women do not have to keep proving themselves. It is a way of empowering women inwardly. The environment creates a trust which is conducive to developing inner trust. Out of that environment women leave connected with inner sources of power which perhaps they haven't connected with before. They don't feel devalued just because they are women. Out of this, networks of conscious women can be formed. Perhaps, for certain women, a day will come when there is an ordained religious order that has not sought permission of the monks to be ordained.

CT: Isn't there the possibility, though, of women becoming increasingly separatist in their worldview?

CF: The emphasis which I give in working with women safeguards against that. Separatism comes out of blaming men. I'm not interested in placing blame. I emphasize very much not wasting energy by consuming ourselves or even concerning ourselves with blame. That places the source and cause of the problem totally with external factors.

CT: Which is to make it a power center.

CF: Yes. Of course. I emphasize that a way of evading participation in that destructive power system is by displacing the responsibility for it, by saying it is *all* outside of oneself. We easily see structures and power centers as adversaries, forgetting that adversaries are given that role by the presence of the victim. On one level, men seem to benefit from the power systems that exist, but essentially everybody loses. Division is detrimental to everyone's well-being. I make that very clear.

CT: In what ways are men losing out?

CF: Any power structure which resists challenge and questioning rests so much on fear, and this breeds tightness, narrowness of vision, and inner alienation. Clinging to power prevents men from an open and receptive way of being, from receiving the feminine within themselves. Such people have to concern themselves constantly with protection, defense, and aggression in order to keep others from participating.

CT: That's a grave situation.

CF: Right. Let me speak further to the issue of separatism. Women's retreats and workshops do not exist as opposite to mixed retreats or male retreats. That's not the purpose of them at all. It is basically to provide a particular kind of environment which emphasizes the maximum degree of ease in communication and inner exploration. For many women, that happens primarily in a single-sex environment, at least at some point in their lives. It is also not separatist because it is not an attempt to create another kind of institution with a leader, hierarchy, and belief system. And that is very important.

CT: What do women experience with each other?

CF: Women learn the fundamental response of opening and not closing off to anything. They learn that women have much to offer each other and bring a balance to the feminine and masculine dynamic. We do not promote the feminine as being superior, but seek to find an inner rapport between the feminine and masculine within.

I don't use those concepts as being purely gender-oriented. They can be evocative concepts. For example, receptivity is usually regarded as a feminine quality but action is regarded as masculine; pliability is regarded as feminine and discipline as masculine; emotion as feminine and intellect as masculine. Everyone holds within themselves all of those qualities, but our conditioning leads us to emphasize one over the other. This often is in detriment to our own balance.

CT: Is wholeness an integration of the feminine and masculine qualities?

CF: Wholeness is mutual rapport, a cooperative relationship between the variety of dynamics.

CT: There is also a diversity of perceptions and values among women about their place in the world. Women have traditional and conservative views with the centrality of their role being focused around the home as a mother and wife.

CF: There's nothing wrong with those roles. I think we must find our place in the world in which we feel free and fulfilled.

When roles are adopted out of insecurity or conditioning, they become not roles but reality. Then it is impossible to grow. "I am a mother and that's all I am." "I am a wife and that is all I ever will be."

When someone assumes a conclusion about one's identity, it safeguards against the insecurity that arises in exploring freedom. We may feel insecure when we challenge our realities and begin to expand beyond the roles. So out of insecurity we hold on to our stated reality.

CT: In other words, if one identifies with a role, one is inhibiting oneself.

CF: You limit your sense of possibility.

CT: Some women will say, "Look, I haven't got any choice. I am house-bound and role-bound. I don't have time or money to go on retreats and workshops or to grow with other women." How would you respond to that?

CF: The physical environment for the role doesn't determine if one is bound. Some women will feel incredibly bound by the role and other women in the same environment will not feel bound at all. The latter are about to explore inwardly their own horizons, their possibilities, and to feel creative. So it's not the role, or the lifestyle, or choice which is inhibiting. It is the degree to which we subscribe to it as our total reality.

The primary factor is a sense of vision, both inner and outer. If there is no inner connection, then the outer becomes all important; the role, functions, positions, jobs, and chores become all consuming. It serves a purpose because it provides a sense of identity and a sense of being needed. If there is an inner connection, the outer doesn't have that emphasis. The role is part of one's life but not the whole of it. We can make our inner life visible in the world. Being a mother can be a strong and direct way of being present and effective in the world.

CT: Being identified with a role can be exhausting.

CF: Inevitably. If there is no inner connection, then many women feel a vast sense of emptiness and loss; an interminable grief when their role becomes redundant. There seems to be nothing left that will make them somebody in the world. What is left is the feeling of being nothing.

CT: Isn't it the same for those who put so much emphasis on career?

CF: Yes. It depends how you use your outer life—whether you use it as a slot to lose yourself in or whether it is an outer manifestation of your inner awareness. With inner awareness, you constantly undergo change. Therefore, your outer life offers up all manner of possibilities so that you're never dependent on career, role, or possession.

There are certain things which contribute to change, but I don't think they are particularly specific to women. Often the factor is crisis. This can come about with loss—loss either through death or rejection, or loss of function or identity. For others, it is a feeling of inner discontent which cannot be ignored any longer. One may stay with an environment where everything seems superficially comfortable and smooth, but inwardly one is unfulfilled. Something is missing. For others, it is the inner vision of an intuition of one's potential as a woman.

CT: How do you see this awakening of women in its historical perspective?

CF: I think it is often inspired by social reality. Just twenty years ago in the West a woman's place was ordained from the time she was born—to be a wife, a mother, and perhaps have a little job on the side. In the 1970s, all that was questioned. Women were then thrown into a new identity crisis, again mostly by outer authorities, and those roles were no longer satisfactory. New expectations were placed on women to be feminist, independent, and strong. This forced countless women into examining their relationship to life and to themselves.

Now the social expectations have changed again. Women

are expected to be superwomen. We are expected to pursue a career, be professional, be financially stable and independent. We should also be good mothers, run good households, and be very competent. It is a combination of the two past expectations. This new identity creates an enormous amount of pressure on women. Women still have to question who they are because of these major changes in expectations in the last thirty years. We have to question who we are very deeply and where we are going in our lives.

> "The face of the ideal woman stares at us all the time. She makes only false and empty promises. She is not a friend to any woman. I can say that to any woman and she'll know exactly what I mean."

CT: Who is setting these standards?

CF: Magazines, books, movies, the media. Who wins the awards for being "Woman of the Year"? The women we see on television are viewed with admiration. Our models are always set up by the input we receive. Ordinary women are constantly being questioned about whether they feel satisfied or dissatisfied with their lives. Women are being forced to keep looking. They must have the space for inner inquiry and questioning.

The face of the ideal woman stares at us all the time. She makes only false and empty promises. She is not a friend to any woman. I can say that to any woman and she'll know exactly what I mean.

CT: What is the impact of that? I was in a shop today and there must have been two complete shelves of women's magazines, each one with a very attractive woman filling the cover.

CF: I ask women, "How many hours during your lifetime do you think you have spent looking in the mirror? Why do you do it?" For most women, it is thousands and thousands and thousands of hours. It's not looking in the mirror simply because the mirror reflects back the image. It's looking in the mirror for the ideal woman. Do I have the right kind of face? Do I have the right kind of haircut? Do I have the right appearance? Do I have the right weight? In the number of collective hours we have spent looking in the mirror, we could have changed the world. We could have changed the whole world with that energy! Most of that energy has been undermining, because perhaps only .0001 percent find the face of the ideal woman in the mirror.

CT: Even those who are regarded socially as beautiful often do not think or feel that they are beautiful.

CF: There's always insecurity, always somebody more beautiful. No one can defend themselves against crow's-feet, wrinkles, and excess fat. No one can defend themselves against their bodies and time. This enormous pressure on women can be useful and not negative when we find ourselves questioning our place in the world. So instead of blindly pursuing culturally accepted role models, women can ask themselves, "Do I want to live like that? Do I want to get hormone injections to have full breasts? Do I want to dress like a man in order to appear professional?"

Women are realizing that imitation of models is not a worthy pursuit. It is not the path to acceptability, worthiness, or fulfillment. Women are caught up in the negative effects because their conditioning is so much oriented around being acceptable and approved of.

CT: What is going to make the shift from imitation of the so-called successful woman?

CF: Women who are successful must question the goodies they get from being successful. Successful women get involved in playing the presentation game. They want to show the attributes of success. On a retreat, I ask women, "How many images do you have about me? Do you expect me to fulfill them? Are you going to model yourself after them?"

CT: Don't we need role models?

CF: We do, but we need role models that are based on actuality, not based on fantasy. It's not good to emulate someone because they seem to have power, authority, control, or spiritual achievement. It is worthwhile to emulate someone if that person encourages you to find a truth about yourself, not to conform or copy what they are.

CT: It is interesting that we do not hear much about the inner feelings and day-to-day experience of famous role models. Actually we have no idea what their inner life is like.

CF: Women who come on retreats express appreciation for having a woman teacher. It is valuable to have a few role models, but I feel women are very fortunate in having very few authentic role models. If you do not have a model, there is no one to tell you this is the proper way to do this, to tell you to do it this way to get a reward, or tell you to follow this way to make progress. Without a model anywhere, you have an enormous amount of freedom. You have no one to say to you, "You're right. You're wrong. You're really progressing. You're doing badly." Then praise and blame from another doesn't really matter. It takes an enormous amount of courage to let go of the outer authority. In many, many ways, it is a very free place to be.

CT: Not having a model is immediately freeing and liberating. But does it contribute to a liberated feeling inside?

CF: Not necessarily. Women have to call on their inner qualities. We have to assume standpoints. If you have no clearly defined path, you are at times going to adopt paths that lead to a dead end. It's very necessary to have the humility to say, "I was wrong," and to start again. It takes an enormous willingness not to assume any standpoints of "I know" or "I am" or "I have." You have to be willing to listen to the feedback of others. It is a hard path for many women, I feel. But women are forming a vision of life which is enormously strengthening and empowering. Underneath their negative conditioning, women connect with life, as they spend time being with themselves and with each other. What I hear from women time and time again is a deep experience and vision of interconnectedness and oneness. If women listen to that and hearken to that, then we don't make so many mistakes.

CT: In other words, to realize interconnectedness is liberating.

CF: Yes. That is what I hear echoed from almost all women. And they know what comes from that is trust and wisdom. The process has its own momentum and is very organic. It's immediately very liberating. It's the source of women's empowerment, which discards negative conditioning.

For hundreds of years spirituality has been at the root of women's vision. It's nothing new. Women have spoken of this realization and vision for generations upon generations. Yet it's totally new for women who discover it, a replica of what women have seen before. Women have an enormous spiritual heritage that has survived every other single tradition. It has never been erased or modified by any tradition, whether Buddhist, Christian, Pagan, or whatever. The same vision has continued despite the differences in conditioning, lifestyles, and externals. In this seeing, women speak with the same voice.

CT: Women's realization of freedom and interconnectedness has widespread ramifications for social, religious, and political realities.

CF: The process is escalating, although its implications have hardly begun to be felt. I feel it is a process from which there is no turning back. It is going to transform every level of our world. I feel the awakening of women is going to change everything.

The New Paradigm

An interview with Fritjof Capra

Fritjof Capra's book *The Tao of Physics* was a milestone in the analysis of the religious and philosophical insights of the East as related to contemporary Western science and physics. Since the book was first published in 1976, it has become an international bestseller.

Fritjof was born and educated in Austria where, in 1966, he received his Ph.D. in Physics at the University of Vienna. From there he moved to France, where he researched theoretical high-energy physics at the University of Paris.

In 1969, while sitting by the ocean one summer afternoon, he experienced "the whole environment as being engaged in a gigantic cosmic dance." He had a sudden realization that the mind of the scientist and the mind of the mystic were not as far apart as one would think. Capra had also been attracted to Zen Buddhism, where the meditative inquiry bore a marked resemblance to the paradox and puzzles of quantum theory. Not surprisingly, he dedicated his first book to such people as Krishnamurti, Alan Watts, and Carlos Castaneda.

The next step took him to California, where there is vast exploration taking place in philosophy, cosmology, astronomy, physics, psychotherapy, Eastern thought, the religious experience, and mysticism. As he went about his research, he began to see a direct correlation between the exploration of the scientist, employing experimentation and hypothesis, and the exploration of the meditator, employing inner observation and spiritual discipline. Capra recalls how a spiritual insight emerged from the depths of his consciousness without any effort or planning. "Coming, as it did, after years of detailed analytical thinking, it was so overwhelming that I burst into tears."

Although he is not a political organizer, he is an avid speaker for the international Green movement. With Charlene Spretnak he coauthored *Green Politics,* which won the *New Options* Political Book Award for 1985.

Fritjof presently lives in Berkeley, California, with his wife and child. He is on the faculty at the University of California and is also a founder and director of the Elmwood Institute, which organizes seminars for the exploration of Green concerns and publishes a newsletter.

It might be appropriate to describe Fritjof as an intellectual visionary. He fulfills an intensely valuable role in the Green movement by pointing out to the scientific, academic, and business communities the failings, if not destructiveness, of old ways of thinking which fragment life into mind, body, and environment. In his book *The Turning Point,* he says that this mechanistic view is an outdated perception. Physics and spirituality share holistic, ecological perceptions—a viewpoint of totality rather than separation.

One of Fritjof's major contributions is that he is able to speak and write to an influential and privileged group of intellectuals within Western society and thus, to some extent, act as a spokesperson for many grassroots activists who do not have access to that repertoire of scientific concepts. In this sense he acts as a bridge between two seemingly polarized perceptions.

•

CT: Could you briefly summarize your book *The Turning Point?*

FC: I think it is the first book that offers a grand synthesis for an emerging new vision of reality, an emerging new paradigm that includes concepts, perceptions, values, and modes of action. I recently had the thought that it may also be the last book of its kind. Parts of this emerging new vision were described in other books, including my first book, *The Tao of Physics*. *The Turning Point* provides an overall grand vision. It has now got to the point where so many people are working on various aspects of this vision with so many new ideas that a summary is no longer possible.

CT: In your books you incorporate perceptions and consciousness, and the way that this affects our whole way of living and being. Since the publication of your book, what steps have you taken to explore ways to implement these awarenesses?

FC: The implementation is my main work now. I am not working on any further elaboration of theoretical concepts, although I have a very theoretical mind. Naturally when I give seminars I have new ideas and I write articles about them. Here at UC Berkeley I teach a course about ecology and peace which I call "Deep ecology—the paradigm of peace." I give lots of lectures and seminars around the country. I also speak to business people, to corporate executives and managers to show them how new perceptions can be applied in the management of business and economics.

Three years ago I founded an institute called the Elmwood Institute, after this area where we live. The institute's purpose is to serve as a bridge between ideas and action. I have come to believe that this change of consciousness could and should happen much faster if we want to avoid catastrophe.

CT: So you are moving away from being a writer to more direct, personal communication.

FC: Yes. This is not an abrupt change. When I wrote *The Turning Point* I had a group of advisors. These people wrote background papers for me and I also had many discussions with them. It was a collaborative effort, although I wrote the book entirely alone. I'm also very inspired by the people who attend my seminars, so I get a lot of material from other people. The starting point is the recognition that the major problems of our time are all part and parcel of the same crisis—a crisis of perception. By major problems I mean the threat of nuclear war, the devastation of the natural environment, the persistence of hunger and poverty around the world. Our social institutions, our politicians, business people, and so on are using an outdated worldview to solve these problems, a worldview which is no longer appropriate. At the same time we are seeing a change of consciousness, an emerging new vision of reality. I describe to them this new vision as it emerges in science and in the various social movements: the ecology movement, and so on.

Our dominant culture is in its decline because it subscribes to outdated concepts and values. In a declining culture people feel that things don't work the way they used to, so instead of changing they go back even further, to old values. The force of this conservative backlash has been stronger than I thought, although Arnold Toynbee and other cultural historians predicted it. The situation is now more critical. The conservative forces are stronger and the alternative forces are stronger. So it becomes important to promote nonviolence explicitly as a essential aspect of the new paradigm.

CT: There is also a noticeable marriage of the conservative forces with orthodox, fundamentalist religion.

FC: The cultural transformation is of such a depth that it cuts through all the fields. So you have the same paradigm shift and conservative backlash in religion. You'll also find this backlash in science. Just think of all the scientists who work for the military. It is difficult to tell if the backlash is gaining momentum. It's hard to make predictions with regard to cultural change. We don't really have a theory of social change.

CT: The alternatives or complementary movements are in the ascendant?

FC: Yes, without any doubt. Let me give you an example. Daniel Ellsberg told me that the Democrats commissioned a series of secret public opinion polls to work out an election strategy. They found that the American people nationwide are very scared about anything nuclear—nuclear tests, nuclear bombs, nuclear waste, nuclear energy, you name it. The media here systematically tried to eliminate the debate about nuclear power after Chernobyl. They sent out the message that this could never happen here. But public opinion went in the opposite direction and people spoke out. What seems like a conservative dominating force may be very shallow. Underneath people get more and more ready for change. So for us who work on new visions and new political ways, this is very important. For example, Christopher, you are not going to be elected when you run for Parliament in Britain as a Green Party candidate, so you have an excellent chance of not compromising and of really telling people the way things are.

CT: Peace, ecology, the women's movement, the influence of Eastern philosophy, the alternatives in medicine, education, science, and technology, the development of psychotherapy—they are all making inroads. At the same time, one also sees a remarkable resistance to change. The media frequently have a critical, if not negative view towards anything that is a step away from the status quo.

FC: This is absolutely true. Speaking for the American situation, the media are owned by industry, as are politicians. Industry and business—the corporate community—have heavily invested in the status quo. They don't want to change it. The media condition people to an incredible extent. However, there are also alternative journals, newsletters, radio stations, and other kinds of programs available.

CT: Concepts and language are, as you pointed out in your books, extremely influential on people's psyches. Just take one concept, *nonviolence*, as an example. As important and essential as it is, I think it awakens in too many minds a feeling of being passive, withdrawn, and fearful. There are millions of voices supporting violence at many levels. I think that what is often forgotten is that nonviolence is to be equated with sustained communication at all costs.

FC: Yes, that's very well put. As we know from Gandhi, nonviolence is not at all passive. This knowledge is now reexpressed and rekindled in the politics of the Green movement. The Greens are clearly nonviolent and have this explicitly in their principles.

CT: Owing to the rapidity of change, concepts get quickly outmoded.

FC: They change faster because the world becomes evermore interconnected with the modern means of communication. It doesn't take so long for a development in one part of the world to be known in another part.

CT: In England we have a reasonably coherent philosophy in the Green Party manifesto, including such themes as nonviolence, ecological awareness, and grass roots activity, but, at the same time, it remains individualistic.

FC: That's right. The Green movement here is coming together slower because the country is much larger. If you look at the history of the Green movement in Germany you see it begins in cities. The cities there are not far from each other, so things go on locally. Here in the Bay Area there is a group called the East Bay Greens, there are the San Francisco Greens, the North Coast Greens, and the South Coast Greens, and often these groups know little about each other. On the other hand, it is no use at this point having a national organization and a candidate for president. Nothing will change in American politics. We have to be really clear about our purpose. I'm not a political organizer; I'm in communication with the Green movement. I created the Elmwood Institute explicitly for the purpose of providing an intellectual resource base for the Green movement.

CT: In England there is certainly a lack of adequate global

analysis, even though the Conservative and Labor parties have decades of research to draw upon. To what degree is there sufficient reflection, analysis, and publication taking place in Green movement?

FC: Not much in the Green movement, because the organization is just beginning, but people are meeting. For instance, we had a symposium of some thirty presenters and critics of the new paradigm who met together in a secluded place for five days. We explored a lot of different areas and asked a lot of questions. For example: is the term "paradigm" useful at all? Where is the serious research? What are the inconsistencies? What needs to be synthesized? What is the state of the European movements?

> "Ecological awareness is at the very center of Green politics. At its deepest level, this is also spiritual awareness, because ecological awareness recognizes the fundamental interconnectedness of everything. We are embedded in the cosmos as individuals and as societies."

CT: What about the spiritual element within Green issues? How does it compare to the European movements?

FC: It is much stronger here than in Europe. Ecological awareness is at the very center of Green politics. At its deepest level, this is also spiritual awareness, because ecological awareness recognizes the fundamental interconnectedness of everything. We are embedded in the cosmos as individuals and as societies. In this country, the Green movement recognizes that explicitly and therefore tries to incorporate the spiritual into the political right from the start.

CT: From your point of view, what happened in Europe?

FC: Being European, I travel back and forth all the time and so get a pretty clear picture. The new awareness is emerging on both sides of the Atlantic, but it takes very different forms. In California during the seventies, you had the so-called New Age movement—including the occult, humanistic psychology, and holistic healthcare—which was heavily oriented toward spirituality. There was a noticeable lack of political awareness and social consciousness. This phase is over now. In Europe throughout the seventies, the alternative movements were still drawing their energies from the student movements of 1968 and were heavily politically orientated. Many had a Marxist or New Left background. They were much more politically astute, but on the other side they had very little notion of what it was to live a healthy life. They managed stress very badly. There was also a noticeable lack of connection with spiritual values.

CT: Why?

FC: In Germany the combination of spirituality and politics has a Nazi flavor, so it was to be avoided at all costs. Now the situation is slowly changing on both sides. Californians are becoming more astute politically and the Europeans are becoming more spiritual and healthier. This moving together is helped because a lot of interchange is taking place.

CT: Greens from Europe certainly come here to the U.S. but what about Green activists going from here to Europe?

FC: The Europeans sometimes feel they can't learn much from the Americans, so they don't invite them. The Americans can't go on their own because they don't have the money. The German Greens, comparatively, have a lot of money because they make money with every election. They run very cheap campaigns and then they get large refunds from the state, so they send people over here on fact-finding tours.

CT: I'd like to shift to the personal level, especially since your daughter was born recently. One of the difficulties we are faced with is how to integrate our global concerns with our personal responsibilities as a parent and partner.

FC: Well, I've just gone through a phase in my life which was very important. My daughter, Juliette, is now eight months old. She was born right here in this room. I spent the first three months entirely at home, not attending to my usual work at all. She has two parents who mother and nurture her. I think this last point is extremely important, not only for the children but also for the parents and especially for men.

During the first few days, I experienced a tremendous appreciation for women. When you have a newborn infant, you can't get anything together. Breakfast before noon? Forget it! It is such an emotional, mental, and physical change. Every two hours you get up. Just imagine that women traditionally did this alone and then not just with one baby but two or more. Other women were involved and supporting, but now with nuclear families many women have been doing it alone.

A baby becomes a connecting point with anybody. When you have a baby with you, you can connect with people at the purely human level. Race, religion, male, female, age—none of that seems to matter. For me, I'm very eager to have intellectual discussions, organize them, and write about them. But now anybody with a baby is so much more interesting than anybody else. So I really believe that if men got involved with that intensity we certainly wouldn't need a women's movement. And, of course, it would be better for society as a whole.

CT: In that respect a young life is a factor showing our interconnectedness with each other.

FC: We learn a lot, too. [Fritjof is holding the baby in his arms and says to her, "We have been talking about you."] She is still at that stage where she thinks, "He who speaks does not know and she who knows does not speak."

We worked out a schedule where I get up around seven in the morning. From seven until ten I am at home and will help my wife take care of the baby and spend time with her. From about ten A.M. to one P.M. I write. In the afternoon I have her for about half the time. Just before you came I was working in my office and she was crawling around on the floor, so the work is really shared.

CT: As you expressed earlier, the present model of the nuclear family is under incredible threat. There is not the support of the old system.

FC: The nuclear family is a very clever invention of the business world because it maximizes consumption. Each family has a vacuum cleaner and a toaster and a car, or even two cars, and all the other gadgets that came out especially during the fifties with all that technological optimism. If you want to see it cynically and in an exaggerated way, in order to maximize consumption, they put people in little concrete blocks. In the sixties, there was a reaction to all of this with the starting of the communes. The communes didn't work very well. They were not supported by the surrounding society, although a few of them did quite well and are still functioning. There is much to be done at the local level.

CT: Thank you for including your personal and social life along with your ecological awareness in this interview. Thank you, Juliette, for listening and being so patient.

FC: She will now eat the microphone to conclude the interview!

An Alternative to the Madhouse

An interview with Father Benedict Ramsden

When Benedict Ramsden was in his early twenties, he lived with his wife, Lilah, in a remote village hamlet in the middle of Oxfordshire, England. One evening he and his wife "invited God to take over their home." God was appointed landlord and they offered their home for the use of anybody that came. The very next night, a sick, broken-down man who was totally soaked through from a rainstorm knocked on their door and asked for shelter. Lilah told me that God had "taken up our offer immediately. We couldn't believe it."

That first knock on their door set the pattern for the rest of their lives. The suicidal, the schizophrenic, the abused, the lonely, the violent, and the fearful have taken refuge in the home of the Ramsdens. They have been brought by doctors, nurses, social workers, and family members and friends. Some of those who live with the Ramsdens have come straight from the mental hospital, or the clinic, or from the terror of a violent household.

Benedict attended Keble College at Oxford University, where he studied theology. Afterward, he became a priest in the Russian Orthodox Church. His journey to the Church began when he was just two years old, during World War II. During the war many people were sent from the city to stay with families in the countryside, which was thought to be safer from Nazi bombs. An elderly woman stayed at the Ramsden home in Oxfordshire. She was a Russian Orthodox Christian and prayed daily before a lighted icon in her room. This was the first of a number of important contacts that he would have with the Orthodox Church.

After university, Benedict and his young family moved to Willand in Devon and once again, their home became a place of refuge where, at times, families in crisis would be sleeping on the living-room floor. Not only did the Ramsdens take on a wide range of suffering adults and emotionally disturbed children but they also had eight children of their own, with an eighteen-year age span.

In 1983, Benedict, Lilah and their children moved to Totnes in South Devon. They persuaded a local bank manager to give them a mortgage on a seventeenth-century family house that was up for sale in the middle of the town, and again left their door open. The local health authorities were quick to take advantage of their skills and the house was soon full. Today, the Ramsdens have gained a reputation for being especially effective working with people classified as schizophrenic, not only reducing or eliminating their drug dependency but also enabling their guests to regain their sense of self-worth and value as human beings.

Throughout the years, Benedict, who is now fifty-four, has been approached many times and commissioned on a number of occasions to write about the work he and his wife are involved in. However, the fullness of the day, which begins at six A.M. with a service, does not give him much opportunity for sitting at a desk. They currently have twenty residents in seven houses. There are also two children remaining at home, by now well-adapted to the impact their parents' guests have on the household. In 1991, the BBC broadcast a documentary on the Ramsdens and their work.

Our meeting was held in the drawing room of his beautiful, old house. The bookshelves are filled with large volumes on the Russian Orthodox Church, religious art, history, and the works of William Blake. Classical records, icons, a television, as well as a VCR and an array of contemporary and antique furniture litter the spacious room.

•

CT: I would like to talk with you about how you are using your home. What is happening in your household?

BR: For about twenty years, my wife and I, along with our eight children, have kept an open door to people who have wanted to live with us. Over the years and particularly for the past fifteen years or so, this has evolved into our caring for people with schizophrenia and related conditions in our home.

For a long time we just looked after anyone who came along. I don't think there was anything particularly wonderful about it. We were probably lonely and just liked letting people into our house. [Smiling] Years ago we used to take in people of all sorts—homeless families, abused and battered children, and people with mental difficulties. People who had schizoid tendencies, whatever they are, seemed to thrive with us. The result was a buildup of pressure from various social agencies for us to take others.

"Mary did quite well with you, so would you like to try with Jane?" In that way the whole thing slowly grew more and more specialized. In a way, that is a sad thing. The law was not terribly interested then and it was possible to mix everybody up in a way which would not be possible under the kind of regulations we have today. It is terribly difficult to bring all sorts of people together in one home.

CT: Where did your training skills come from?

BR: They are intuitive. I'm not a nurse, doctor, psychiatrist, or psychologist. It would appear that my wife and I have a knack at handling a certain kind of person. Or probably we create an approach or space for a person to have the chance to do some flourishing.

In the past twenty years there has been a move in Britain toward community care of the mentally ill. For years and years they were buried in vast baronial mansions built in the last century about four miles out of towns and cities. Those places had a once-beautiful name, "asylum," which over the years was changed by those very places into something terrible. Then came a new idea, one with which I am in complete agreement. Instead of pushing the "mad" out of society, perhaps the place to look after them is in it.

Unfortunately, the implementation of this scheme coincided with a shortage of money as well as with a shortage of time because many things had been put off too long. One might even think, the way things have gone in some places, that the whole policy was created in order to save money. You can't push the so-called mentally ill into a community that cannot cope with them. You must first change the community and that takes a lot of time and a deliberate policy of education and preparation.

People from Russia, for example, think our society is unspeakably shocking in the way we treat our old people. We herd them into special ghettos—old people's homes—and eventually into

> "In many cultures . . . the mad have been regarded as, perhaps, touched by something beyond our normal experience. They were treated almost with veneration. But for years our society has herded them out and hidden them."

hidden places, unmentionable and unfaceable places. In our culture no one wants to know about dying or death.

East Europeans are also shocked about the way we treat children. They just can't understand us. In many cultures, as probably once in England, the mad have been regarded as, perhaps, touched by something beyond our normal experience. They were treated almost with veneration. But for years our society has herded them out and hidden them.

We reject these people in a special way which we make look like kindness. We dress up what we are doing by giving it a much nicer name, so that for instance, banishing an old person to a ghetto for the senile is called "giving them peace and quiet." But it's really the habit of euphemism at work. We call something by a nice name in order to pretend it doesn't exist. You may notice my use of the word "mad." I do so deliberately because it avoids a dangerous euphemism. There is a right way of using the expression "mentally ill," and the model of a mental illness has its uses and its truth. But the concept is dangerous when taken literally.

CT: Contemporary social thinking puts people into categories and fixes them in a particular way. What is your experience of people who are classified as mentally ill or schizophrenic?

BR: They display symptoms like hearing voices, having visions, feeling a control from outside, withdrawal from relationships, paranoia, and so on. I don't intend to deny the reality of any of these symptoms or of a link between them. But I do wonder to what extent we should regard them as sick in themselves. For example, we talk about people who are labeled schizophrenic. This is a vague umbrella word we use when someone who has had a mental breakdown exhibits five or so out of about thirty different symptoms. Yet we use it as though it refers to something as specific as measles.

Of about one percent of the population who break down, the symptoms are the same all over the globe. But in certain sorts of societies nearly all of that one percent become disabled. Their lives become a total tragedy. Very significantly, in other societies the proportion of these same people with these same predisposing factors is much, much less. It is obvious that schizophrenic breakdown depends not only on factors in the patient but also on factors in the society around. In a highly competitive and demanding society, where everyone must prove his or her worth, breakdown is much more likely than in one where dignity is afforded a person simply because he or she exists. To have a schizophrenic personality in our sort of society is an almost certain damnation to catastrophe. For example, our society has very little time for people with artistic temperament, or for someone who isn't into making money.

The fact is we need all sorts of human contributions to society.

CT: What is going to change the consciousness of people when the community is so competitive?

BR: We need to learn to accept others for what they are and not for what we think they ought to be, to accept what they can offer and not what we think they ought to offer. And we certainly won't learn to accept people unless we meet them. I moved into this house six years ago. At that time the law governing the activity that I am engaged in was so vague as to be almost nonexistent. I bought this house and I just moved in with a rather large group of people. No one in the street took a great deal of notice, though it must have been obvious that a few of these people were perhaps a little bit odd at times.

Two or three years ago, vast mental institutions were closed and people were dumped on an exploitive market. So Parliament passed legislation aimed to give local authorities a weapon to clobber people who were exploiting the unfortunate by packing five into a room in order to get money from the state. The new law said that a house with three people or more in it who had at any time been mental patients had to be registered as an institution. So I had to apply for planning permission to register.

Usually in such circumstances the neighbors hit the roof. "Good God, they are going to open up a lunatic asylum next door to my house! The value of my property will slump!" In my case, they were reassured that all I was doing was getting retrospective permission to do what I was already doing. Then most of the people on the street sent letters of support for my planning application. Our neighbors had ceased to think of "schizophrenics" and thought instead of people as themselves, the individuals they knew, not as members of any category but as persons. Now that outcome is unusual. Normally you hit an enormous wave of opposition.

I haven't taken people out of a big lunatic asylum and built some modern little lunatic asylum in the middle of the street.

I'm just living my own life with my family in our own house and sharing it with other human beings. Our guests may have certificates to say they are dotty. In fact, they are not all that much dottier than me. No one stops to think that these people have in the past been locked up in high security units at the cost of nearly 1,000 pounds [1,900 dollars] a week.

CT: Isn't it dangerous for you and your family to befriend these "eccentric" people?

BR: The people I have here need a bridge back to society. This is an alternative to the madhouse, the lockup. I have people who were in very high security situations indeed. They are brought into this house, some of them having just come, quite literally, from locked cells. They are let into this house with everything that's here to be thrown around. It's obvious that there are dozens of things around the house that can be used as a weapon for attack, that there are precious things which can be broken. The moment they walk into this room they are at once impressed by someone having a totally different set of expectations of them. There are no straps, no pads, no heavies or hypodermics at the ready, and the room hasn't been cleared of possible weapons. They walk into a beautiful English drawing room which contains some beautiful things. Not only are they being met with trust, to them it seems like a princely sort of room and they are being treated like aristocrats.

CT: Atmosphere can't protect you and your family from latent patterns of violence and suicide. How do you deal with that?

BR: I can only say that no one has ever hurt me. I'm the most awful coward. I couldn't do this if I really thought I was going to get hurt. In whatever way I tackle the aggression that crops up, it is not going to be by a head-on show of strength. I might get hurt!

And then I've got children. Most of my younger children have grown from babyhood with this work going on around them. They too have not been hurt.

When someone comes into this room, they see there are several things to throw around. I'm giving into their hands the power to hurt me. Because they have that power given them, they do not need to seize it.

I also give them the right to be angry. I think that anger is a proper part of human makeup. If you really hold anger down, you are heading for trouble and likely blowups. Human beings must have space and opportunity to be angry.

For instance, I had a young man who came here. Just a few days before he came it took five men to remove him from where he was and most of them were hurt, some quite badly hurt, in the struggle, and these men were heavies, the sort you use as bouncers in a nightclub. They were the bouncers for society. Now, I had read that young man's history and I regarded that young man's anger as legitimate, so I gave him the opportunity to express it.

If he was really angry, my wife or I would simply join in with him and do whatever he was doing, shake with him or struggle with him or just cuddle him. We would say, "Of course you are angry." We would take him somewhere where he could have a good scream. Or we would go caving together [hike through nearby caves]; there he could go through some deep experience like fear or anger. If I was feeling really brave, I might have a wrestle with him.

There is a lot of aggression and competitiveness in people which can be converted into play. In fact it is in play that most of us learned how to handle our aggression. I'm not talking about games like playing cricket with its highly ritualized structures, but about much simpler levels of play, like arm wrestling or Cowboys and Indians or just tousling about on the lawn. But people can't handle it when it's linked with anger. People won't get into those situations with "dangerous people" because they are afraid of getting hurt. If you go into those sorts of situations and regard it as a game, then the person isn't presented with *your* fear and anger. Then you get some very different results.

CT: Doesn't this require total acceptance of the person?

BR: I wouldn't say total. My acceptance is extremely imperfect. But they are more than willing to accept me on the same terms that I accept them. I accept them as they are and I don't pretend that I am not a mess myself. Perhaps I am prepared to be more accepting than some people are. Even then I show them that my acceptance is a mess, too. The person can feel that he or she belongs here and has a right to be here. It is quite rightfully not a peaceful situation. This is a place where you can bring your anger and your lack of peace. You can shout about it, swear about it, beat your fists on the ground, or talk about it if you want to. That evaporates a lot of the violence that surrounds it. I think it is an unhealthy suppression of anger which makes us violent. What is important is coming to terms with the fact that we, with all our frustrations and with all the anger that stems from them, have a right to be here.

CT: Here on Earth, here in life.

BR: Yes, here in existence. You don't qualify for being here by being accepted by others, by matching up to some model of behavior, however generous that model. The whole of existence is an extraordinary mystery . . . or a meaningless nonsense; that's a possibility that we all live with. But even then, it is a chaos out of which the most extraordinary visions of order can come from time to time.

I happen to believe there is a little more than chaos to it. I believe that every human being is some unique vision of something significant. I don't know what that something significant is. I think you have to meet people as they are without trying to impose on them your understanding of what they are. Then people don't feel threatened in their very existence. I think metaphysics is nearer to the surface in people than we imagine. Something so precious is perceived as being forced into a stereotype and so the person instinctively reacts. When a person sees clearly that he doesn't fit into the stereotype, and that people are going to bring all sorts of force to make him do so, even to the point of cells and straps and drugs, I'm not surprised that violence is sometimes the outcome.

CT: What takes place when a person has left the institution and he or she walks through your front door to meet you and the family for the first time?

BR: Nothing very dramatic. The very first thing that happens is a slightly middle-class reception. Someone brings tea, coffee, and biscuits. We all sit around on the sofas in this beautiful room. It is all a bit stilted. I'm painfully shy and very conscious of the experts who have come with the new arrivals. I am very aware of their curiosity about how I am going to handle things and so I get more and more inhibited.

The nurses, social workers, and doctors go away and we start doing things without thinking. We'll probably just pile into the kitchen and get the next meal, involving the new arrival at whatever level he or she can be involved. We would certainly bring them into something ordinary and something with an element of enjoyment in it. For example, the day after the violent person I just spoke about came, we went caving.

Some people thought it was a bizarre thing to do with him. The caves are about six miles from here in Buckfastleigh. We went through a series of caves used by the Royal Marines to test men for personal selection. The course is said to quite often reduce the average Marine to tears. At the other end of the cave, the Marine might come out shattered. For the first time in his life, he has been underground and is really frightened through being stuck here and there for a few minutes. He finally comes out with a surge of adrenalin and sheer relief and excitement and he splashes around in the icy river to wash the mud off. My lot have just done the same and no one can tell the difference. Royal Marines and lunatics look exactly the same! And I'm not making a cynical point.

CT: That experience would dissolve differences.

BR: There is a parallel to that in the home. Homes aren't places of tranquility. You know a family is a pretty abrasive atmosphere for growing. We don't run some marvelous saintly vision of the way a Christian home ought to be or something like that. If my wife and I are going to have a row, we've learned long ago how good it is to have a row in front of the people we look after. Let them see that the world isn't divided into two classes, the professionals who wear white coats and sit behind desks and never have emotions, and the "mad" who have all the emotions. Anger wells up from time to time between my wife and me, and this is part of how the real world is. For some of the guests here, this is an extraordinary recognition. Some of the people that come to me have been in a mental hospital since childhood.

One woman here had been in the hospital between the ages of nine and twenty-three. All the emotion she would have seen, except for some exasperation from the staff, would have been regarded as "mad." It is for her an extraordinary experience to see ordinary people's rows and their emotions, and then the patching up and the forgiveness and the carrying on of the relationship. What we are doing here is so ordinary that there's hardly anything to say about it. We are letting back into ordinary life people who for some very odd reason have been pushed right out of ordinary life by our society.

CT: How many people come to stay here at a time?

BR: We look after a total of eleven people, some in this house and some in another house run by friends of ours who are trying to repeat our methods. Years ago the Social Services would ring us up late at night and say, "We've got a homeless family. Put them up on your floor or we'll have to split them up." The house was crawling with people. It was enormous fun. Now the law has changed and one wouldn't be allowed to live in such a lovely way.

CT: What is the result of closing down the mental hospitals and sending people back into society?

BR: I've watched it go all wrong. It is a national disgrace. People are committing suicide all over the place. Having spent up to sixty years in a secure surrounding with constant room temperature of seventy degrees and three meals a day arriving punctually, they are then thrown out into some bed and breakfast or some lonely rest home. People are killing themselves or dying of trauma. It is an appalling national disaster and no one wants to know about it because we don't concern ourselves with the "mad." Certainly asylums are misused, underfunded, and understaffed. But there are some people who need shelter, need an asylum in the best sense of this beautiful word. But in the midst of all this disaster I have also watched, at first hand, a lot of people who have gained tremendously from being integrated into the community.

CT: What about the homes being built for those coming out of incarceration in a hospital?

BR: The authorities so often build a little community project to house the mentally ill, costing a million pounds or more and staffed with a team of professionals. Yet it is built so much on the model of the old one that there is no breakthrough into a new understanding. It is simply a mini-lunatic asylum in the middle of the town instead of a maxi one outside it. Oddly enough, because it is small, there is sometimes even less room for humanity. At least in a big institution there are usually places to skive off into and be human.

Because I have a religious label, some people assume we are working some kind of white magic or spiritual healing or that we have some peculiar gift. They can then dismiss us as an exception. Recently we decided to repeat what is going on here. We set up another house with a couple who said they were willing to let people into their home. Most of it is intuitive and it really takes a conscious intellectual effort to describe what we actually do. Our methods, so far as they can be said to be methods, are being repeated there and are producing the same results.

CT: People come here to stay and experience a normal household. Isn't there a reluctance for people to leave? Don't you have a stable population?

BR: People come here first of all on an experimental footing. That isn't determined by time. Eventually there comes a mutually recognized time when they say they want this to be their home and when we say that is okay with us. Then they have more or less the same rights as our own children. No one wants their children to hang around their necks until they are senile. But if you want them to go away, first they must be secure. Once secure, they can take risks and leap off. We make this commitment that if you go away, even if it's after a blazing row, you can always come back here. You may not leave in some ideal state—"Brother, you are cured. This is the great day that we wave you off." You may be a mess when you go away. But whatever terms you go away on, you may always come back. The place is not locked up. You can let yourself in, help yourself to some food, find a bed or mattress. The house belongs to you.

> "One of the really heavy things about our society is that it doesn't believe in enjoyment. It doesn't believe in joy. Although it pretends to, it doesn't believe in pleasure."

CT: Doesn't that get abused?

BR: It gets abused sometimes. Sometimes people decide that this is just a place of asylum and all they want to do is stay here. To a certain extent that is all right, but obviously we hope for more. The world out there is pretty rough and painful. But there are a lot of attractions and once people have the confidence, these draw them out of the parental home. It is restrictive to live in a parental home with Big Daddy and Big Mama. We've got our style and that inevitably cramps the style of our children and everybody that lives with us. There is the great draw of girlfriends and boyfriends in the world out there. It is no use to give them six months to build themselves a bridge to the outside world. It would be like being sentenced to death. A child will leave when he or she has the confidence, because the world out there is seen as enjoyable.

CT: So is confidence the key?

BR: Perhaps the key is enjoyment. One of the really heavy things about our society is that it doesn't believe in enjoyment. It doesn't believe in joy. Although it pretends to, it doesn't believe in pleasure. We really do think there is something questionable about it. And certainly the mad are not entitled to enjoy themselves.

CT: What is the difference between joy and pleasure? Isn't the primary interest for millions the pursuit of pleasure?

BR: In trying to make a distinction, I don't wish to imply any rejection of pleasure. By joy, I suppose I mean those kinds of happiness that understand even misery. That's joy—when you can march happily into the mouth of a lion. And it starts with the simplest pleasures. Every step of joy is a step in the direction of something utterly profound which makes the courage to exist possible. So right from the start we encourage people here to enjoy themselves. Joy draws you out beyond the limits of what you are in. So here I am trying, through enjoyment, to point the way to a much larger vision.

CT: There are no visible symbols of religion here.

BR: You are wrong. There are icons all around. There is quite a big one, called "Joy Unexpected," as you walked in. You are making a point though. While Christianity is not concealed, it is not pushed at you. You don't get a lot of God talk in this house. For one thing, a lot of people who have come here have latched on to God talk as the language of their madness. Take for instance this symptom of being controlled by external forces. For some people, such hallucinatory forces are seen as God or angels or, of course, devils. God language and popular religion is so damaged by puritanism and so bound up with guilt that it has actually become dangerous, particularly for many of those who come to be with us.

Some, for example, have never adjusted to the discovery of their physicality and, in particular, their sexuality. They are not able to love themselves and accept themselves in that sort of way. When that is linked up with morbid guilt and popular puritanism, then God talk becomes extremely damaging. I think there is too much God language around already, and one forgets it is a very inadequate language that tries to give sound to silence.

CT: Do you have any kind of ritual or services here? Do you dress as an orthodox priest?

BR: I dress most of the time in ordinary clothes. But not always. If I'm going to be in a situation where it is appropriate, I dress in the traditional dress of a priest. I do it much more naturally than I would, say, dress for dinner, and I don't regard it in any way as embarrassing or disturbing. There is a chapel at the heart of the house. Services are held there at six in the morning. If anyone wants to come, they have to get out of bed. There is no reward for coming. If people come to the services to get approval from us, they soon discover things don't work here in that way. There also isn't a pressure to keep people away. If it were one side or the other, I would lean slightly toward discouraging people, simply because of the dangers for some.

CT: What does "spiritual" mean for you?

BR: It describes the fundamental resource for me to lead a life in which I'm not afraid of what most people are afraid of. There is some kind of peace here, in the middle of something very chaotic, which can be communicated by a kind of silence. You can live, have fun, fool around, and still convey that you are rejoicing in your existence, which is perhaps the most fundamental thing a religious person does.

CT: So out of the silence comes rejoicing, enjoyment, and play.

BR: And also forgiveness. Forgiveness has got linked up with guilt and being "let off," rather than with love and being allowed to "grow up." I think forgiveness happens before you do wrong rather than afterwards. In an odd way, we have the right to be wrong. Children in their own home have the right to be naughty because being naughty is part of growing up.

Acceptance is to allow people to exist in their own existence. Forgiveness is something like that. We could have an argument, of course, as to where forgiveness stops and sheer condoning of evil begins. Forgiveness is some sort of generosity that allows people their mistakes, their failures, and their dignity; and with God, that generosity is infinite.

CT: In the process of growing up, children are quite often self-conscious, especially when bringing friends home. Have any of your children said, "Look, Mum and Dad, do we have to have these people with us all the time?" Have they been accepting, if not forgiving, of your open house policy?

BR: Of course they have. Any child who survives their childhood is only able to do so because they have learned forgiving. I can say that there has been very little negativity. My grown-up children, like all children, will occasionally complain about their childhood. Parents must expect to be clobbered with what they've done to their children. But mostly my children say they didn't realize how extraordinary their life was until they went to the homes of other children, which, they say, seemed very boring compared to their own. My children have a fund of the most extraordinary stories.

I remember my teenage son bringing home a new girl-friend. At the time we had someone living with us who was very disturbed and had a habit of wailing and screaming. She used to think that the house had become a ship which was sinking. And she would run her fingernails down doors. She didn't open the doors, but just liked to scrape behind them. My son was making his girlfriend coffee late at night in the kitchen. Behind the door there was this extraordinary howling and scratching going on, which my son treated as though it wasn't there. It was like in *Jane Eyre*, where Mr. Rochester's mad wife is kept in the east wing. There in our kitchen sat this poor girlfriend, with eyes as big as saucers, not quite daring to ask, and my son didn't explain it for hours. We all thought it was awfully mean, but he thought it was rather funny.

> "One thing my children are not frightened of is mental illness in themselves or others. They have met madness and death and so they do not go around in a state of dread, wondering what these things would be like if they were to turn up."

All sorts of other "mad" things go on in our home—I'm allowing here for the word to be used in all sorts of nice ways. Living in this madhouse has enriched our lives and, for the most part, our children will say the same for themselves too.

One or two very old people have died here and that too has been enriching, and the children have mourned their loss as much as my wife and I.

CT: Have your children missed out on anything?

BR: They have missed out on some of the orderly quietness of average suburban life. But then they have also missed out on much of the tedium. I would say one thing my children are not frightened of is mental illness in themselves or others. They have met madness and death and so they do not go around in a state of dread, wondering what these things would be like if they were to turn up.

CT: What would you say to someone who genuinely wishes to explore ways and means to accommodate people on the fringes of society?

BR: I'd say, please do. In our case, we learned as we went along. One has to purify one's motivation as one goes along. I think that especially one must be very wary of picking up vulnerable people in order to boost one's own lack of inner security.

CT: What kind of people are suitable to house eccentric people?

BR: Well, I'm very struck by the fact that I live in a town with a hippie-ish element. I know it is an old-fashioned word to use. I have eleven people who are helping me with this work and nearly all of them have this alternative element about them. Now, a lot of alternative people don't fit into the work structures of ordinary society. They get pushed to the fringes of it and aren't much valued. It offers them not much more than the dole. Yet these people, who are not interested in a highly competitive way of living, often have a kind of laidbackness which could be opened out into a welcoming attitude that is needed for fostering. Economically, this would be marvelous because of the real saving in pounds and pennies to the community. The savings in terms of human happiness would be extraordinary.

CT: Why doesn't this happen?

BR: Because it involves risk, and one of the ways we justify excluding the vulnerable from society is by claiming that we are protecting them from risk. It will only happen when society is willing to face these rejected people. We have to learn to take risks with them just as we take risks with our own children and so-called normal human beings. Inevitably there would be a few mistakes but truly this is a way forward.

What I would like to see is a sort of fostering scheme in which there are people with no remarkable skills but who have an ordinary level of acceptance of humanity. What we are doing is something like that, and it isn't really anything remarkable. It could be repeated a thousand times over. When you think of those whacking great hospitals that held four to five thousand people all closing down and almost nothing to put in their place, and then look at the sheer waste of these noncompetitive people—many of them could do such a lot of healing.

The Greatest Danger We Face
is Our Denial

An interview with Joanna Macy

Joanna Macy, an American Buddhist scholar and teacher, is primarily interested in applying the principles of Buddhism to situations that we face on a day-to-day basis. Not surprisingly, one of the main themes in her work is interdependence. This theme emphasizes unity and support among people rather than the isolation and powerlessness so predominant in our societies today. Joanna has said the root problem in dealing with issues is this sense of powerlessness. She is committed to bringing about a fundamental change in the psyche so that we experience a sense of power and can express that power in a caring and loving way.

Several years ago, Joanna realized that as a human being, woman, and mother, she was experiencing deep feelings with regard to the present planetary crisis. Through her communications with other women and men she realized that these feelings were quite normal and not limited to a handful of particularly sensitive people. Drawing on her wide experience in meditation, psychotherapy, and general systems theory, Joanna began facilitating workshops called "Despair and Empowerment" for people concerned about the state of the planet.

Her workshops include a number of exercises that aid in releasing a whole variety of emotions including fear, joy, anger, rage, love, hurt, and gratitude. Through allowing the range of feelings and shared experiences to flow, another level of contact and communication with the whole of life is revealed. What comes out of these workshops is a clear release of fresh energies and a sense, to varying depths, of solidarity with people and planet.

In her book *Despair and Personal Power in the Nuclear Age*, Joanna writes, "Despair and Empowerment work helps us to increase our awareness of these developments [threat of nuclear war, the progressive destruction of our life-support system, and the unprecedented spread of human misery] without feeling overwhelmed by the dread, grief, anger and sense of powerlessness that they arouse in us. These feelings are largely suppressed and this repression tends to paralyze us. We need to help each other to process this information on an effective level."

In 1979, Joanna founded Interhelp, an international network of people concerned not only with peace and social justice but also with transforming personal perceptions that inhibit people's capacity to respond effectively to global realities.

In the late seventies, Joanna became interested in the Sarvodaya movement in Sri Lanka. She wanted to know more about these people living in the villages and applying Buddhist principles to all areas of their life, including health, education, agriculture, and the arts. In 1980, with the help of a grant from the Ford Foundation, Joanna went to Sri Lanka for a year. She wrote *Dharma and Development,* which describes her experiences in Sri Lanka, their influence on her, and the nature and purpose of the Sarvodaya movement.

Joanna, who was born in New York City, now lives with her husband, Francis, in Berkeley, California. They have three grown children, Peggy, Jack, and Chris. Her latest book is *World As Lover, World As Self.* In October 1986, she flew to England to lead a Despair and Empowerment workshop and to give the annual Schumacher Society lecture in Bristol. She stayed at my home in Totnes and there we taped the following interview.

•

CT: There has been a general conception that men are superior to women, human beings are superior to creatures, creatures are superior to trees and plants, plants are superior to rocks.

This hierarchy has been created in the minds of people. How can we look at this world in a fresh way?

JM: We can start with our bodies. We are made of the dance of organic molecules produced through an action that goes back so far that we can say we are starstuff evolving. This is a wonder, a miracle. I look at my hand and I see four and a half billion years of life on this particular planet. I look at that with awe. I behold you, Christopher, that you are a product of this particular planet in a medium-size solar system off to the edge of this galaxy. Innumerable adventures have molded what you are, what I am.

CT: The body is a remarkable composition. Sometimes that observation arises spontaneously. Is it useful to explore and reflect on the interdependence of the body and world?

JM: Yes. We need to be aware of that. We also need to be aware of the fact that we are appearing in this postindustrial culture after a millennium of conditioned thought where matter is viewed as less worthy than mind, where it is viewed even with some contempt or disgust. A dichotomy has been posited between mind and matter and one set above the other.

CT: Do you mean that we have reduced matter to the whims of the mind?

JM: In our culture, conditioned by Newton, Descartes, and the so-called Western Enlightenment, the relationship between mind and matter has always been a puzzle for us. You have those who say that only the mind is real and matter is not. On the other hand, you have those who say only that which you can touch, weigh, and measure is ultimately real. The Jungian psychologist and thinker James Hillman points out that materialism is often a product of the mind's fear of matter. Matter, *mater*, mother.

A paradoxical dynamic gets set up when you polarize mind and matter. When you do, then the goal of the spiritual path, whether it's to be enlightened or saved, becomes the extraction of mind from the toils of matter. You see that in a number of religious traditions. And when you try to escape from that which you are dependent upon, a love-hate relationship gets set up between the ego, mind, and matter. Matter of the natural world is seen as a trap. You may try to be very austere or ascetic in order to extract yourself from matter, or else this love-hate relationship leads to a materialistic drive to dominate and acquire.

> "When the Buddha talked about greed or grasping, he mentioned four objects. The other three were all mental: grasping after ego, grasping after views and being right, and grasping after rituals."

CT: A materialist or hedonist might say, "It's not a trap. I like matter. I like things. I want more. Why shouldn't I get more?"

JM: Four-legged creatures, for the most part, don't eat more than their bodies can assimilate. They don't get sick from overeating. It is the mind's greed that makes us want to acquire more than we can use. Materialism is the greed to acquire. It is really a mental phenomenon. Money is a beautiful example of this. You can't eat that piece of money, or wear it, or make love to it. You can't sing songs to it, or hear it, or walk in it, or smell it. It's an abstraction, an example of a kind of psychosis. When the Buddha talked about greed or grasping, he mentioned four objects. The other three were all mental: grasping after ego, grasping after views and being right, and grasping after rituals.

CT: A person may say, "I am aware of this grasping, but the awareness doesn't seem to stop it or even brake the force of it."

JM: We are taught that we have a lot of needs. Our culture, conditioning, and advertising tells us how we need to look or smell. Ivan Illich, the writer on contemporary society, talks about the creation of needs for our capitalist system. It is very easy to fall into the illusions that our needs are many. Here mindfulness can be an extremely important and powerful friend. As Gandhi said, "The world has enough for everyone's need but not for everyone's greed." We can then begin to experience the freedom that is here for us when we liberate ourselves from socially induced needs.

CT: So one important aspect is mindfulness and awareness of our mental condition. Elevating ourselves over nature is assumed to be the true reality. How can we individually and collectively contribute to dissolving this division?

JM: Consciousness is co-arising with physical and mental experience. There isn't a consciousness all by itself in a pure, rarified, absolute state. Consciousness always has an occasion for its presence. We are therefore continually in dialogue with our environment. We can never be a disembodied monad; we are products of interaction. We only want to be free when we feel trapped by nature. Life is a dance that we can enjoy, and it is quite wondrous. We exist in interplay, in interaction. Our senses tell us that. Each sense gate or faculty of seeing, hearing, smelling, tasting, and touching tells us that we are engaged in interaction.

CT: In your work and travels you meet women and men who are looking at the global situation and experiencing a great deal of personal pain as a result of what they see. Would you say they are perceiving this in the world, or is the world mirroring a state of mind?

JM: I think it is being perceived in the world. And I'd like to say that I have yet to meet anyone who is not in grief over what they see happening. Anyone who is conscious today sees that there is hunger, that there is inequality and progressive destruction. Anyone who is to any degree awake to the conditions of the world knows we cannot count on there being a future.

CT: That includes the people you have met in the East.

JM: Many in the East and in the Third World have immediate survival issues uppermost in their mind—feeding the family, getting shelter. Among affluent Westerners this suffering appears as awareness of a kind of global pain. It does not necessarily depend on one's politics. It is even felt among those who say they aren't interested in reducing armaments or in the decimation of the rainforests. Everywhere there is a dis-ease, a malaise, a grief that we cannot count on there being a future. I think for most people this pain for the world is barely conscious; it is seldom discussed. There is resistance to painful information. So when painful information is offered about the effects of Chernobyl or another nuclear accident, or the spreading of the deserts, or the poisoning of the seas, for example, people block that out. That's a self-protection mechanism, to protect the mind from fear, especially the fear that the mind will lose control. "I can't bear to think about this because I might get stuck in despair. I might shatter into a thousand pieces. Don't ask me to take it in." There is fear of experiencing the pain that goes with this information.

CT: So how do you respond to someone who comes up and says, "I can't take it anymore. I can't take this pain that I see all around me?"

JM: I invite them to breathe. In my workshops I use a breathing method which is 2,000 years old. It comes out of the early Tibetan tradition and was originally used to help people develop compassion. That's really what we are talking about. We are talking about suffering *with* our world. And to suffer with our world is literally what compassion means.

CT: Are you saying, "Don't close off to the pain."

JM: Yes. To close off to the pain is to go dead inside. It is a form of death. I believe the greatest danger we face is our denial—thinking that we can't look at the dangers—in economics, in the environment, or with the military. We imagine we are so fragile that if we look at what's happening we'll break.

CT: But it takes courage to open up the heart and mind to the pain of the planet. Where is this courage going to come from?

JM: I think it is quite easy. That's why I prefer to work in groups. We need each other in this. This is a very natural process for us. We are made to be open and interactive with each other. Just look at my hands or my eyes or ears. As human life evolved on the planet we became more vulnerable to the world. We evolved sensitive protuberances. What we are made for is to connect. Just as the cells and the neurons in our bodies are made to connect with each other and spin complex systems, so are we. This, I believe, is the teaching in the *dharma*.

> "We tend to feel that we cannot take in any grief or problem unless we have the answer to it. That's backward. We have to expose ourselves to a situation, stand naked before it, so to speak, before an appropriate response to the problem can arise. "

We are made for interaction. By using the breath, for example, we can experience the taking in of information about the planet without breaking down.

CT: What is the breathing technique that you use?

JM: Focusing on the breath, you note the sensations that accompany it, whether at the nostrils, throat, or lungs. You watch the breathing in a very alert way, like a cat by the mousehole. You begin to notice that you're not breathing by a choice of will but that you're being breathed by life. Then you picture the breath as a stream of air coming up through the nose, down through the throat, lungs, and then out again to link with the living, breathing web of life made up of all beings around you.

When the images of suffering come to the surface of your mind, you allow that pain, like a dark substance, to be carried on the breath stream into your very being and through your heart. You don't hold on to it but let it flow back out into the healing resources of the web of life. You are simply allowing yourself to be present, letting the pain pass through your heart. That's all you are asking yourself to do.

CT: So there are three important reasons for compassionate breathing. One is to give ourselves greater capacity to deal with the suffering that we hear and see every day. The second would be to deal with the accumulated suffering and pain. The third is that the breathing helps reveal our organic intimacy with life, interdependent and coexistent.

JM: Yes. And I would add another. During the Vietnam war, our president, Lyndon Johnson, said, "Don't bring me a problem unless you can bring me a solution." We tend to feel that we cannot take in any grief or problem unless we have the answer to it. That's backward. We have to expose ourselves to a situation, stand naked before it, so to speak, before an appropriate response to the problem can arise. Breathing in this way helps us, quite literally, to stop putting up an armor against bad news and to allow it to connect more intimately with us.

CT: When you give a public talk, I would imagine that a number of listeners block out some of the things you say, as they would in other situations.

JM: Actually, I don't find much resistance. Once people allow themselves to engage in a practice, even a little bit, it becomes self-validating. Often, at a big gathering, people are invited to do a version of the Four Abodes: loving-kindness, compassion, joy for others, and equanimity. An awakened human being expresses each of these heartfelt abodes without effort. I could just stand up and talk about them, but that would be quite dull. So I prefer instead to invite the people to turn and use the person nearby as a meditation object. I then talk them through an exercise so that each of these four abodes can be experienced as they behold this other person. This is a practice that people can take away with them. You can do it sitting on a bus or looking across to someone at the checkout line at the supermarket. This is a way to practice deep interconnectedness.

CT: If, as you say, the greatest problem is the denial of global realities, then the opening of the heart and exploring other ways and means to do that would be of primary urgency.

JM: It is. It also directly addresses the sense of being overwhelmed. When one looks at what is happening to our air, our water, our people, our planet, one can feel overwhelmed. What can just one out of nearly five billion people do except shut down or try to divert oneself? I like to emphasize that compassion has two sides to it. There is the side of opening to our pain for the world, which is compassion. The flip side is joy in each other's joy, power in each other's power, synergy. We can train ourselves to look at other people—be they lovers, friends, or strangers—as resources. They are people from whom we can draw intelligence, love, ingenuity, for we are in the web of life *with* them. We can't solve the situation alone. We solve it in synergy with them. This can be experienced as a form of grace.

CT: In opening the heart and working with the pain, there comes about a flow of energy towards healing the planet and oneself. One begins to participate in that flow. But what do you mean by "grace?" Where does that grace from?

JM: I just love thinking about grace. It's hard to talk about it with our limited language. In Japanese, there are similar terms, *jariki* and *toriki*, which mean "own power" and "other power." Grace is the realization that you are part of something larger and receiving from it. You are carried by this realization like a wave carries you when you are surfing. You don't need to dredge up out of your own meager resources all the love, patience, courage, and inspiration that you are going to need. It's there in abundance. One of the first times I had a sense of grace was when I was going off to Sri Lanka. Some friends of mine came to say goodbye to me. I was going there for a year and I knew that I would be lonely. I knew there would be situations I would face that I wouldn't have an answer to. Together we invented a little ritual which we called "the web." It evoked my own creatureliness as part of the web of life. My friends spoke out, rather poetically, about things in the web which they wanted me to be aware of. One would say, "Joanna, I give you the gift of the diving trout, who is unafraid of the dark. May you be ever fearless of the dark." Another said, "May I give you the gift of the song thrush, who lets its voice be heard. May you never be fearful of speaking out." These gifts were with me throughout the year.

In the Christian tradition in which I grew up, grace has come, by and large, to be equated with God's action—the experience of God holding me in the palm of his hand, the everlasting arms buoying me up. But grace can come just as well through other people. In the practice of the Four Abodes, people can open to resources that come through others and are beyond what they think about themselves. For example, when I see your courage for what you have chosen to do with your life, I could say, "Oh my, Christopher has more courage than I." It would make me feel rather cowardly, which is a great foolishness. Or I could look with the mind of grace. The courage you show is in the web of life which called me into being. And I rejoice in that.

CT: So what emerges from the heart is appreciation free from comparisons.

JM: And free from envy. Grace is the power of life abounding around me that I can open myself to and channel. You don't have to stop and ask, "Was that *my* idea or *your* idea? Was that *your* courage or *mine?* These views become irrelevant. It's courage *happening.* It's ideas *happening.* It's love *flowing.* Because it happens in the interaction, it doesn't belong to anybody anyway.

CT: In the dynamic of this connectedness and interdependence we keep making contact with those giving support to life.

JM: Precisely. I would say that is one definition of grace—giving support to life. People can look at each other with great sensitivity to the other's pain but also with exaltation. They can look at each other and laugh and be happy knowing that there is a circulation of vitality that brings courage. You begin to dare to do things.

CT: With the sense of others, there is a wider view.

JM: That's grace.

Pruning the Plum Tree

An interview with Thich Nhat Hanh

When the United States government sent in hundreds of thousands of troops to wage war on the people of Vietnam, Thich Nhat Hanh, a Buddhist monk, was leading a contemplative life in the Vietnamese tradition of Buddhism and running a School for Social Services. Thich Nhat Hanh, known as Thay [teacher], began to speak out about the war and appealed to the North Americans and their allies and the North Vietnamese and the Vietcong to enter into peace negotiations.

He and his students, who were committed to serving the people in the villages, found themselves wedged between the two warring factions. The American military believed they were puppets of the Vietcong and the Vietcong believed they were stooges of the American armed forces. Some of the young men working for the School for Social Services were summarily executed for refusing to take up arms. They experienced food shortages and harassment from those committed to change through violence.

Thay became one of the first major voices in Vietnam to call for the withdrawal of the American forces from his country. That was in 1967. He launched an appeal for a ceasefire while on a visit to Washington; his plea fell on deaf ears. The war was to escalate even further and to include neighboring Laos. The widespread bombing of Kampuchea led to a holocaust, with the loss of two million lives. Compared to the tragic holocaust of World War II the Western world largely turned a blind eye to the immense sorrow of Kampuchea, Laos, and Vietnam. None of the North American leaders or military were brought to trial as war criminals.

It was impossible for Thay to return to Vietnam. Other monks, nuns, and laypeople, including coworker Sister Cao Ngoc Phuong, had to flee Vietnam. The year before he was assassinated, Martin Luther King, Jr. nominated Thay for the Nobel Peace Prize. In the years following Thay's arrival in the United States, he and Sister Phuong traveled the world campaigning for peace in Vietnam. He was chairperson of the Buddhist Peace Delegation in Paris during the war.

Since the end of the war in 1975, Thay has continued to travel extensively, giving retreats and workshops for adults and children in the West. He has extensive contact with Vietnamese refugees, both those from the war and the boat people. He has written many books, including the bestselling *Being Peace, The Miracle of Mindfulness, The Heart of Understanding, The Sun My Heart,* and most recently, *Touching Peace.*

Thay is a former vice-chair of the highly respected International Fellowship of Reconciliation and a member of the international advisory board of the Buddhist Peace Fellowship. He is widely loved throughout the peace movement.

One of his poems, "Please Call Me By My True Names," has been widely reproduced. Commenting on the poem, Thay says, "I have many names and when you call me by any one of them I have to say 'yes.'" This is an extract from the poem.

> Do not say that I'll depart tomorrow
> because even today I still arrive.
> Look deeply: I arrive in every second
> to be a bud on a spring branch . . .
>
> I am the mayfly
> metamorphosing on the surface of the river,
> and I am the bird which, when spring comes,
> arrives in time to eat the mayfly . . .
>
> I am the 12-year-old girl, refugee on a small boat
> who throws herself into the ocean
> after being raped by a sea pirate,

and I am the pirate,
my heart not yet capable of seeing and loving.

My joy is like Spring, so warm it makes flowers bloom.
My pain is like a river of tears,
so full it fills up the four oceans . . .

Please call me by my true names,
so I can wake up,
and so the door of my heart can be left open,
the door of compassion.

I met with Thay in Plum Village, Bernac, where he lives in southwest France. For a month in the summer, Vietnamese refugees and Westerners spend time together. Meditation, mindfulness practices, informal discussion groups, and spiritual teachings make up the daily life for some 200 men, women, and children. Thay loves children. My daughter Nshorna, who accompanied me to Plum Village, recalls with joy, as I do, her contact with Thay and Sister Phuong. In talking with Thay, I sensed in him a profound goodness and kindness that has not been desecrated by the violence and pain which he and Sister Phuong have witnessed.

•

CT: Refugees from Vietnam and Laos come to spend time with you. They are dealing with major upheavals. What do you say to these refugees?

TNH: They have problems that they carry with them and they have problems of living in a strange country. So I address their real problems. They may have lost someone dear in their homeland or during the trip if they are boat refugees. Their father, mother, son, or daughter may have been killed during the trip. They come with a wound within them. Their new country is so different that they have to struggle. Sometimes they cannot integrate, but the children can. That will be a problem too. It leaves a gap between themselves and their children—a generation gap and a cultural gap. Refugees often want to retain things that they consider to be precious, beautiful from their culture. Their children don't want these things, may not understand them, and are fascinated by the new culture. Parents worry that their children will be dragged into the negative things. Life here in the West is also very busy. They don't have enough time for their children, so they are losing real contact with them very quickly, and the children lose their parents very quickly too.

CT: You must hear this many, many times from refugees you visit in France, Britain, Australia, and North America. What do you say to a family wounded, suffering, and in conflict?

TNH: I respond by trying to help them understand the causes of their suffering. I propose ways of spiritual practice so they can be relieved of their suffering.

CT: What comes to mind when you think of the causes?

TNH: There are so many causes. They suffer if they keep thinking of the past. I tell them, "There are many beautiful things in the present moment. You must learn not to cling to what is no longer present. Face life in the present moment." I teach them how to be in touch with life so they enjoy what is positive in the present moment.

CT: Some parents and grandparents wish to retain something of the old culture. How do you respond to that? There is something to be let go of in the past, the old, yet there is something to be included?

TNH: These things can be described as their cultural heritage. So, when they leave the refugee camps they still have these treasures. They must make good use of these things, like a traveler would, carrying with him or her something on his or her journey abroad. What they think is beautiful and valuable can be applied to their new life. Children can see the beauty of their heritage, receive it, and put it into their new life.

CT: As you know, the young become very much impressed with contemporary Western culture. They may regard the older culture as being foreign or distant. Where is the bridge for the young to their cultural heritage?

TNH: I recommend that parents show equal interest in Western society as do the children. I say to the parents, if you don't understand Western culture you will not know how to trust it. I ask, "What do you consider to be valuable in your own culture?" Your culture should be translated in a form that can be understood and acceptable to your children who are growing in this environment. Culture is the way of living your daily life—the way you walk, the way you eat, the way you treat people, the way you live in your home. There is a Vietnamese way of living and a French way of living. You have got to know about the French way in order to tell your children the best elements in that culture. Refugees have to know the elements not worth adapting to. You compare that with your cultural heritage. You can point out to them what you can learn from the old cultural heritage and what you can learn from the Western culture.

CT: What is useful in our culture? What do you think is questionable and needs to be changed?

TNH: The undesirable elements in a culture bring us suffering. The desirable elements bring happiness, help us grow as individuals, as a family. To get in touch with people you find out what makes them happy, what makes them unhappy, and you go to the foundation of that happiness and of that unhappiness. The undesirable element of Western culture is individualism, the belief that happiness is an individual matter. This can be seen very clearly in this culture.

The cultural heritage of the West has not been renewed to provide young Western people here with what they really need. More and more flee their own tradition and look for something else. It is like growing plum trees. You should know how to prune the branches that are not necessary, otherwise they will take all of the sap. In a culture, it happens that there are branches that take over the place of other branches. When these branches grow too much they destroy the tree itself. People must have the courage of pruning, which is somehow painful. If you can prune, you leave space for the tree to bear fruit. That kind of pruning has not been achieved in Western culture, so it creates a lot of suffering. For example, the foundation of the family in the West is no longer solid. Christianity is not providing that foundation, that continued support.

> "People must have the courage of pruning, which is somehow painful. If you can prune, you leave space for the tree to bear fruit. That kind of pruning has not been achieved in Western culture, so it creates a lot of suffering."

CT: By using the metaphor of the tree you demonstrate that there is continual expansionism in Western society without realization of the value of letting go and refinement. Is the expansion of materialism and consumerism what you have in mind?

TNH: Yes. People here want more and more and more. They believe that happiness is the satisfaction of always getting what they want. They don't see that this consumerism destroys their happiness.

CT: How would you describe and speak of happiness as distinct from getting what one wants, from the pursuit of pleasure?

TNH: The sole pursuit of pleasure brings about displeasure later. If we have a deep understanding of pleasant feelings, we know that it is not really pleasure that nourishes us. There are other pleasant feelings, that can never harm us, that do nourish us and help us to grow.

When you sit here you feel the breeze. You are with nature, with the healthy elements of life. That kind of pleasure is not destructive. But when you consume alcohol you know that, although it is a pleasant feeling, it is destroying your body and your nervous system. If we only think of pleasure without seeing the nature of the pleasure, then we will suffer.

CT: This requires the ability to discern happiness and pleasure, to understand what contributes to growth and what contributes to our harm.

TNH: We should not be afraid of our natural pleasurable things. Let us realize that these pleasant feelings can only help us grow, make us happy. When we are happy, we make other people happy.

CT: Could I relate that to the issue of refugees? Refugees wish to retain their culture, their beautiful traditional values which give happiness but which don't bring harm. There is often a lot of public debate suggesting that people from traditional societies who have come to live in the West have become too isolated from the mainstream of society here—Muslims, Hindus, Sikhs, Buddhists, and various ethnic groups.

TNH: Beauty has universal values. If you know that, you will make your values acceptable to other groups. The old culture may need some transformation in order for it to become accepted in the new culture. It is like traditions of cooking that belong to a culture. A dish in India imported to France should be transformed a little bit in order to fit the French taste. There are Indians who live or are born in France who prefer another version of the dish. I think if the elements of an ancient culture remain exactly the same in a foreign land it would have less opportunity to be accepted by others.

CT: Does this apply to the Buddha's teachings?

TNH: We need new forms of language to give the message of the Buddha on the Four Noble Truths.

CT: It is sometimes thought that Buddhism is somewhat disengaged from life, from various social concerns. I was a Buddhist monk in Thailand and India from 1970 to 1976. It certainly appeared that way at times.

TNH: In some forms of spiritual practice, Buddhism will look like withdrawal from life. To me, Buddhism should be engaged in order to be called Buddhism. The teaching is to solve problems, not to take you away from life. Therefore teachers have to address real problems of society and of individuals and propose practical ways for people to see into the nature of undesirable situations. To me, if Buddhism is not engaged in social issues it is not real Buddhism. A religion which is not useful will vanish. Buddhism needs renewal. In the history of 2,600 years of Buddhism there have been many attempts to renew Buddhism. I see that Buddhism here should be different. Buddhism should be distinguished from culture. Buddhism is very often mixed up with a local culture.

CT: Don't your robes indicate a culture?

TNH: Yes. To me, Buddhism should be made of elements of the local culture. To build a house it is better to take your materials from the local forest. Essentially, building the house is the same everywhere. I have been encouraging Buddhists in the West to make good use of elements within Christianity and Judaism. I don't mind at all if people chant the Heart Sutra with a Jewish liturgy. It is easier to move the hearts of people with local elements of their culture.

CT: But many people do not feel any association with orthodox Western religion. Many adults here have no history of religion or churchgoing. Some people in the West claim they have no relationship at all to any religious tradition.

TNH: The seeds of tradition are in the blood of people. People cannot be without culture and a tradition, although they may hate it. Sometimes they say, I don't want to have anything to do with my father. But they are a continuation of their father. Thinking is one thing and reality is another. We should encourage them to turn to their culture, because their roots are there. They are not really uprooted. Westerners are still rooted in their culture. They can discover the values in their tradition. Buddhism can be a kind of stimulus to help them to feel rooted again. So, my voice is not telling you to leave your culture. I say the opposite: go to your culture and be happy. That is my approach.

CT: In Western religious culture, the word "God" is a central element in the religious fabric. In Buddhism, we do not use the word "God." Buddhism could be thought of as atheistic. How do you view that in terms of bridging the gap between different religious cultures?

TNH: I think it is better to present Buddhism not as a religion. I think it is important to present the Buddha as a teacher. In Christianity, there are theologians who can think of God not as a person but as the ground of being. Ground of being is something like the *Dharmakaya* in Buddhism. More theologians today have contact with Asian religions, where they seek a language to express elements that have been neglected in Christianity and Judaism. We serve as stimuli in order to help them to bring these things out. We also say that the "mind" is the artist that draws the world, draws happiness, and draws suffering. If we are in touch with the deepest level of our mind, we will discover a source of joy, of understanding, of happiness—so Mind is God.

When I speak of nonduality I say that the rose and the rubbish "inter-are." This is the very heart of Buddhism. The organic gardener takes care of the garbage. He is not running away from the rubbish, because he knows that the garbage will bring the flower back. So there is no gap between the ultimate and the practical.

CT: Dharma teachings embrace the duality of the rose and the garbage. Your teachings explore ways to understand and embrace both the garbage and the rose.

TNH: Yes. In us there is a rose and there is garbage. We should not be afraid of the garbage in us. The moment we accept that, we have peace. We are peaceful because we know how to accept and use these experiences. We know that we can learn ways to transform them so the rose goes into garbage, and the garbage goes back to rose. We are not afraid, we know the techniques, so we can live peacefully without fear.

CT: In the teachings, you encourage people to smile. Some listeners don't quite understand this. Why is smiling important to you?

TNH: When there is a pleasant feeling, you know there is a pleasant feeling.

CT: But you are smiling to introduce the pleasant feeling—not just feeling it when it arises.

> "If you use all your time paying attention to what is wrong you lose the opportunity to get in touch with what is *not* wrong. You have to practice joy also."

TNH: In the *Discourse of Mindfulness of Breathing,* the Buddha said "to feel happy." Smiling is only an expression of that, to make it concrete.

CT: A person might say, "But if I'm feeling sad and I smile, I am not being true to my feelings."

TNH: Smiling alters the body—particularly your mouth. Something happening in the spirit can be translated into the body. But we don't allow that. What is happening in the body will have an effect. Practice mouth yoga, smile like that, and suddenly you have a pleasant feeling. Mouth yoga is what happens in the realm of the body and then a pleasant feeling will be born in the realm of the spirit.

CT: You are saying that by introducing a pleasant feeling into the body it naturally communicates into one's heart.

TNH: Yes. There is a change in your spirit. The body has the right to initiate these changes. Then you can even smile to your suffering. If you smile to your suffering you increase your strength. You are being compassionate to yourself.

CT: The power of the pleasant feeling in the smile is to transform the spirit, the inner life. Isn't there the danger that in smiling we may lose the critical faculty?

TNH: In Western psychotherapy and Western medicine, you pay attention to what is wrong. If you use all your time paying attention to what is wrong you lose the opportunity to get in touch with what is *not* wrong. You have to practice joy also. So we practice to be aware of suffering in order to transform it. We also practice to be in touch with the joy in order to become strong. You take vitamins with the medicine. This is only to reestablish the balance. If a bamboo is too dry on one side and you want to correct it, you will overbend it a little bit so it will become straight.

CT: You are saying that Westerners are too much involved in suffering, too much concerned with what is wrong.

TNH: Yes. Too much suffering kills the spirit, makes your heart become a stone. Everything requires balance.

CT: Do you think there is a danger of becoming saintly, so that we neglect an analysis of major social, political, economic, and environmental issues? Where is the relationship between being warm and caring, and looking into the global problems which are serious for our planet?

TNH: Personal problems are connected to the social, global problems. Psychotherapists know that society is creating more clients for them but they have to make time to heal society, so it does not create so many sick, unhappy, and confused people.

CT: Doctors and psychotherapists make people well only to send them back into the society which made them sick to begin with.

TNH: Yes. We have to begin at home. In the family, you have to look into the problems of your son, daughter, husband, wife. Through these people you see society. Dealing with the family means to deal with members of society. If you practice mindfulness and awareness, you ask your children to be careful about the garbage. When you throw banana peels into the compost heap you experience a pleasant feeling. You know that the banana peel can be recycled as a lettuce. If you throw away a plastic bag with mindfulness you know that it is different. The feeling is uneasy. The plastic bag will take much more time to go back to being a lettuce. When you throw away plastic diapers, they take 400 years to dissolve into the earth. If you are aware that nuclear waste is a kind of garbage, then you feel very, very concerned because it takes 250,000 years to recycle. Considering garbage is to be involved in social action. That affects your children and their children. Generations of families will be affected by the way we use our garbage.

CT: There is a small but growing active public awareness of these problems. Can you differentiate between spiritual awareness and mindfulness, and conservation awareness?

TNH: Mindfulness is the moment you begin to see clearly. The insights have an impact on our behavior in the domain of family life and social life. We find out ways to awaken people. I think that Buddhism in the West should ally itself with groups like ecologists, feminists, psychotherapists, peace activists. We can learn from them and they can benefit from our practice of awareness. An ecologist is someone aware of what is going on in the realm of ecology. So she is practicing Buddhism, she is a friend of mine, she can teach me many things. I can support her in the practice of mindfulness and bring the techniques of Buddhism to her. We can have such a relationship with psychotherapists, peace activists, feminists. They are all future Buddhas.

CT: It is understandable if other societies blame the West for its long history of colonialism and consumerism. What can enable people to understand Western culture without being angry and resentful?

TNH: People in the West accuse themselves as well. We must demonstrate that a simple lifestyle can be very happy. That is about the only thing we can do to help. When the West tries that kind of life, they can get rid of their worries and their depressions. The West needs to *believe* we can be happy consuming much less.

CT: Yet many people throughout the world wish to imitate the West, to take the path of consumerism. They say it is easier for us to let go of consumerism because we have had it. They say, "But we haven't had it, we have to go through this stage."

TNH: We accept each other much more easily if we understand each other's suffering. This is the core of the Buddhist practice; leading a simple life is only one aspect. Look deeply in order to understand the other person. When you understand, you are moved by their suffering. We must try to listen to each other, including children, in order to understand the problems and suffering of each other. That is very helpful. Then we bring out our own experience in dealing with suffering. We exchange experience. We shine the light of dharma on suffering. We transform our being together into a kind of workshop, where we can crystallize a number of methods so that we may share what we learn with other communities.

The Immense Intelligence
of the Rainforest

An interview with John Seed

"I am protecting the rainforest"
    develops into
"I am part of the rainforest protecting myself"
    develops into
"I am that part of that rainforest
recently emerged into thinking."

The above words of John Seed, the founder/director of the Rainforest Information Center in Lismore, New South Wales, Australia, have been widely quoted by ecologists and environmental activists.

Since 1979, John has been involved in the protection of rainforests, especially tropical rainforests, throughout the world. He is a firm advocate of deep ecology—a movement which holds that human beings need to undergo a profound change in consciousness toward living on the earth. He says that when people see through the layers of anthropocentric (i.e., human chauvinist, self-cherishing) ways of living, a most profound change in the perception of life begins to take place.

John employs a fourfold emphasis in communicating the ongoing crisis of the rainforests, in which every year eleven million acres are destroyed for the sake of human convenience. First, he stresses the importance of increasing public knowledge of the plight of the rainforests through the written word. Second, he supports active participation in boycotts and in nonviolent protest, either in the forests themselves or at offices of the industries responsible for the destruction of the rainforests. Third, he engages in active dialogue with the businesses and governments involved. Finally, he holds public meetings and workshops that employ teaching and communication aids, meditations, spiritual exercises, and rituals.

In 1986, John coproduced with Jeni Kendall an hour-long documentary, *Earth First,* on the history of the struggle for the Australian rainforests, a film available on video from their Lismore office.

In 1987, he organized and led the first Australian "Earth First! Rainforest Roadshow." The roadshow gave twenty gigs in twenty nights along 1,500 miles of the east coast of Australia. There were also three "Council of All Beings" workshops and rituals to awaken people's hearts, minds, and bodies to their roots in the tropical rainforests tens of thousands of years ago. In the meditations and exercises, groups experience their ecological being as life elements in common with all other forms of life elements. People share songs, poems, and other experiences, moving toward perceiving themselves as "leaves on the tree of life." The roadshow raised about 7,500 dollars for rainforest activists in Ecuador and the Solomon Islands. In 1992, John went on a tour of the United States and Europe conducting these workshops.

John has also coauthored *Thinking Like a Mountain: Toward a Council of All Beings.* Currently, he is editor of the *World Rainforest Report.* He has helped establish rainforest action groups in Australia, USA, Japan, Europe, and in Third World countries, where most of the rainforests are found.

Prior to 1979, John was a student of Buddhism and insight meditation. He participated in a number of retreats in Dalhousie in the foothills of the Himalayas during the mid-seventies. Upon his return, he moved to what is known as the "Rainbow Region" of Australia, the northern part of New South Wales. There was a migration of so-called hippies to this area, since land was cheap and available. Numerous small communities were started up.

John helped found the Forest Meditation Center and Bodhi Farm, a 160-acre piece of land at The Channon, near Lismore. Bodhi Farm has gained widespread publicity in Australia in recent years for its successful campaigns for the rights of small communities.

The interview with John was held one morning in Sydney while traveling to the airport through the morning traffic. I was on my way to the Rainbow Region, and John was holding meetings with city-based activists.

•

CT: Why do you feel that it is important to preserve the rainforest?

JS: I think it is essential to protect the earth's ecosystem, and the rainforests are the most dense collection of genetic material and species in the world, with over half the world's ten million species of plants and animals living there. It's not really more essential to preserve the rainforests than to preserve species generally. The rainforests are a symbol for all species, a symbol for genetic diversity.

There is also the nonanthropocentric reason. The rainforests are worth preserving because they exist and they have the right to exist and for no other reason than that. We appeal to people to consider that these species have as long and illustrious a history as our own species, having all evolved from a common ancestry about four and a half billion years ago. We have no right to terminate other species.

Another reason is within a human frame of reference. Here, too, there are many reasons not to exterminate species. Every species is part of the same web of life of which we are a part. There is no separation between us and the rest of nature. To damage nature is to damage ourselves. To think we can damage nature without doing harm to ourselves is to misunderstand who we are.

CT: How would we damage ourselves?

JS: There would be a spiritual damage. There would also be a direct material damage to ourselves because the food, building materials, industrial products, and medicines that we depend on don't exist in isolation from the rest of nature. As we wipe out our wild genetic ancestors, we wipe out food and medicine that the rainforests provide for us now and in the future.

For example, where a new disease comes along to blight one of our crops, the only way that we can preserve that crop is by going out into the wilderness to find the wild ancestors of that crop to look for traits which are able to meet that new threat, whatever it is. Crops and vegetables are highly vulnerable to any kind of change in climate and to other environmental changes. They are also vulnerable to the parasites and predators that are evolving. Our crops have to keep evolving in order to continue to exist. Large stocks of wild genetic material need to keep evolving. We can't duplicate life in the laboratories.

> "At present we are consuming those thousands and millions of years within a few generations. Within this time, we will have consumed all of our 'future.'"

CT: What is the present degree of damage or destruction to the rainforests, and what areas on the earth are most seriously affected?

JS: There is some controversy about the degree of destruction. Projections based on satellite photographs show that within the next thirty years all remaining accessible areas of rainforest will have been damaged or destroyed. There is no forest anywhere not being destroyed at an immense rate, especially in Central America, South America, Africa, Southeast Asia, and the Pacific, where most of the rainforests exist.

CT: Who is destroying these forests?

JS: We all are—due to the products that we consume and the lifestyle that we lead. There are two basic problems. On the one hand, there is the standard of living and rate of consumption in the so-called developed world, where masses of people are living in a luxury that no king or emperor could have dreamed of a couple of centuries ago. Basically, people are consuming the future. We *could* consume in a sustainable way. We *could* consume the increment of what nature produces without consuming the capital—the capital is the species and the non-renewable resources. We *could* imagine ourselves continuing to evolve for hundreds and thousands or millions of years into the future. At present we are consuming those thousands and millions of years within a few generations. Within this time, we will have consumed all of our "future."

On the other hand, there's the question of the growing population in the so-called underdeveloped world, where huge areas of forests are being destroyed by slash-and-burn agriculture to meet the needs of the rising population and rising material aspirations as well. No room is left for wild nature to continue.

CT: To protect the rainforests, there has to be a real change in our attitude in the West and elsewhere to our relationship with material wealth. A brake also has to be placed on population growth. As individuals, how can we work with these major global issues?

JS: My whole life is spent trying to answer that question. I would suggest that a fundamental change in consciousness right through the human species is necessary. For instance, for fifty-one percent of the human species to make the change wouldn't be sufficient. Basically, an evolution of a collective understanding of all people is the only basis for a resolution of this situation. Reforms are useless. There are no other measures that are going to be of any use at this point because the rate of destruction is so fast and the momentum of the whole human enterprise is so immense that there can be no temporary victories, such as declaring a particular rainforest as a national park. None of those things are of any real use.

CT: So the change cannot be made just by legislation. There has to be a change in the consciousness of human beings toward an awareness of their relationship to the earth. In Judaism and Christianity, that emphasis isn't so much present. How can a Christian look at this new way in the light of his or her Christian beliefs?

JS: There is a very interesting paper written on this subject called "The Historical Basis for the Environmental Crisis," by Lynn White Jr., an American professor of history. In this paper he lays the blame squarely at the doorstep of Judeo-Christian basic creation myths, which say that the planet was created for the benefit of human beings. "They will be in fear and trembling of us" and all the rest of what is found in the Bible.

CT: In Genesis it says, "Man shall have dominion over the earth."

JS: This is the kind of problem we are faced with. It is not so much that everybody still believes this, though many still do, but rather the whole basis for our culture is inextricably corrupted by such unecological beliefs. There are Christians, particularly the fundamentalist Christians in America, who believe in the literal truth of the Bible. I would say that this belief system is among the most dangerous that exist on earth.

A prime example was James Watt, who was the Environment Secretary in the Reagan administration. When he was asked whether we should not be saving some of these non-renewable resources for future generations, he expressed his opinion that there were not going to be many future generations, before the coming of the Lord. Watt said it was really our duty to use of the bounty that had been given to us. He seemed to be saying that there was some morality dictating us to continue to use up these resources!

CT: I attended an eco-theology seminar in Totnes. One of the participating American professors, who was a Christian, said the basic relationship of the creator with the creation is that human beings are, in fact, cocreators with God. Our responsibility is to develop a caring and sensitive awareness of our relationship to the earth.

JS: I feel that is an important step, but nevertheless we need to go further than that. That perception still contains the same sort of basic humanistic arrogance of the human species. It is similar to the notion that we will now be copilots of spaceship Earth. It means there is nature and there are human beings who have the right to direct and control nature. Such beliefs fill some people with great pride, whereas it fills me with immense horror. We have already damaged the earth. Having destroyed the natural life-support systems, we may have to construct replacements. Soon, perhaps, we will have no choice but to be copilots of the Earth, where we will have to create the oxygen, create the clean water, create the cycles that bring us nutrients and break down the waste.

CT: How can we look at our relationship to the Earth and to nature and the materials of the Earth in a balanced way?

JS: I think there are a number of answers to the question "how." First we can internalize the understandings of ecology and biology in the same way that we have internalized these other strange creation myths. I don't think that there are many people who really believe in the idea that an elderly gentleman with a white beard created the world in the year 4600 B.C. But so many actions are based on that kind of outlook.

How do we internalize insights about the Earth? Well, meditation is one useful approach. For myself I have found that direct action in defense of nature has had the strongest influence on me, because in demonstrating to others and to the media, I was also demonstrating to myself a certain kind of commitment. I felt a great change took place in me as a result of placing myself in a stressful situation where I was in danger—in danger of being arrested, of being branded a criminal, and of being judged.

CT: How did the Rainforest Information Center come about?

JS: I was living at Bodhi Farm, a meditation community at Terana Creek in northern New South Wales. A rainforest conflict developed in our watershed only five or six miles from where we were living. I can't recall why we went to see what was happening, but most of my community went and we were profoundly influenced by what went on in the next few weeks. We engaged in direct confrontation with the forestry commission of the state of New South Wales to try to stop the logging. We blockaded their equipment nonviolently; we camped there for a month, and hundreds of people were arrested. That was in 1979. Some people climbed up into the trees that had been marked for felling. They put their lives in danger in order to demonstrate ostensibly to others, and most importantly to themselves, the degree of commitment they felt for the life processes and what was threatened there. One friend of mine spent six days up in a tree hanging in a kind of fishnet. As the bulldozers went past, they'd strike the tree. His life was certainly in danger.

"What I like to do is to lie down in a rainforest, when it is dry enough, and cover myself in leaves and twigs and try to remember my *own* history. From such a forest, less than five million years ago, my ancestors emerged."

A temporary halt was called to the logging and an inquiry took place. The inquiry didn't come up with a result that suited us, though. It was sort of rigged by the person who was conducting the inquiry, who was chosen by our opponent, the Commissioner of Forests. We abandoned the inquiry before it came to its conclusions and we went back to direct action in the same mountain range, Mount Nardi, a few miles farther up. That was in 1981. We spent four moths camped up on the mountain. Then an opinion poll was conducted, after months and months of headlines and television news. It seemed that we had successfully got our views across to the people of New South Wales. A poll conducted by the National Trust found that about seventy percent of the people wanted an end to rainforest logging, and then the government legislated. So the area we were protecting passed from forestry to national park. Six or seven other areas were declared national parks in New South Wales at that time as well.

CT: Few people, however, live anywhere near a rainforest. Even fewer people have ever stepped inside one. People do not have any sense of the awesome beauty of the tropical rainforest.

JS: I think it would be a good idea to try to spend some time in a rainforest, particularly in a meditative state of mind. What I like to do is to lie down in a rainforest, when it is dry enough, and cover myself in leaves and twigs and try to remember my own history. From such a forest, less than five million years ago, my ancestors emerged. I try to allow a reconnection with the immense intelligence that exists in that sort of forest. It gives rise to my intelligence and five million other kinds of intelligence as well.

CT: When you go into a rainforest and cover yourself with leaves, what kind of feelings do you experience?

JS: At the time I don't really experience much at all. Afterward, when I come out of the rainforest and take stock of my life and what I am doing with it, I feel very clear. I don't get distracted easily from the work I have to do to communicate my concerns in trying to protect the rainforest and other natural systems around the world. There is a Dr. Seuss children's story called *The Lorax*. It's about a creature that pops out of the stump of a tree that has been cut down. The lorax says, "I speak for the trees as the trees have no tongues. I'm telling you, sir, at the top of my lungs . . . . "

I was in the Solomon Islands campaigning to save the rainforests there. All of the people in the Solomon Islands are Christians of one denomination or another so it was necessary to try to find a Christian context in which to explain the work that I was doing. So I said that in the Bible we are told that God created the world in five days and it was on the sixth day that he created humans. The first five days were spent creating all of these marvels and humans were created on the sixth day after the rest. If we destroy what God spent five days creating then surely this shows an immense disrespect to God. I don't know if that communicated to the people.

Another way is to see the rainforests as the Ark within which the creatures continue to exist. The logging which takes place can be compared to pulling the planks from the ark to use for timber, an inappropriate use of the materials. Only in the ark can the animals and birds continue to survive on earth.

CT: In other words, by touching people's deep religions beliefs you hope to affect their perceptions of their environment. Why did you choose to go to the Solomon Islands?

JS: It was the result of an invitation I received at a victory party to celebrate the stopping of the logging on the Nightcap Range and other rainforests in New South Wales. I met a man from the Solomon Islands. He had come to Australia in search of help to protect the rainforests in his country. The work for the rainforests in New South Wales had just ended after three years of campaigning, so I was available at the time. I found that the large multinationals were basically scalping these most beautiful islands from one end to the other.

CT: Can you name any of these companies?

JS: Unilever is an English-Dutch company. They are probably the largest trading multinational in the world with an annual turnover which is about 300 times the size of the Solomon Islands economy.

CT: In light of what you saw, would you recommend boycotting their products?

JS: Actually they have changed. Since our encounter with them they have become a rather exemplary logging company in the Solomon Islands. They fired their general manager and changed their methods of logging from total clear felling—no protection of stream banks, no ecological sensitivity whatsoever—to standards of logging which would compare with the kind of standards we are used to in a country like Australia.

CT: Is this good propaganda and publicity put out by Unilever, or have you actually witnessed the change?

JS: We have witnessed the change. The forest department in the Solomon Islands has said, "Please don't attack Unilever. They are an example to the rest of the logging companies in the Solomons."

CT: What brought about Unilever's change in attitude?

JS: The people in the Solomon Islands think it's because we threatened to publicize what they were doing, which would have caused an international boycott of their products. But, of course, the Unilever people never actually said that to us.

CT: What about the large Japanese interests which seem determined to protect their forests in Japan and go overseas for their wood?

JS: Over seventy percent of Japan is forested and most of that forest is protected. But I believe that the protection is temporary. They realize that they can get wood more cheaply in Southeast Asia and in the Pacific than in Japan itself. This leaves the wood in Japan available for some future time. Some people in Japan feel that their own forests are sacred. The point is, though, that the Japanese purchase nearly all of the timber that is logged on the islands. It may be Unilever that is logging, but the logs are then taken to Japan.

CT: Are there other multinational companies whose record isn't exemplary?

JS: In the Solomon Islands, the companies are mostly from Korea and Taiwan. It is pretty hard to get any kind of handle on them in the way you can with Unilever. In Brazil, for example, the largest single cattle ranching operation is owned by Volkswagen. In order to clear an area of the Amazon for cattle, they lit the biggest forest fire that has ever existed. They cleared thousands and thousands of square miles. Multinationals are diversifying into all kinds of different businesses. The nature of multinational corporations is to go after profit. That is their only criterion. A profit can be make in cattle ranching; the beef market is expanding; so Volkswagen got involved.

CT: What can one do to bring this to the notice of the general public?

JS: I contacted the German Green groups with the idea of producing bumper stickers to put on other people's cars, rather than one's own car, to put out information about what Volkswagen is doing. Hopefully this would decrease the sales of their cars and bring about a change in the company's attitude toward the rainforests. These actions are to create a public awareness.

One of the questions which you asked me was how the necessary sort of change in awareness could take place. That is something which I have been really feeling frustrated with—both the direct action and these kinds of actions with Volkswagen, because at times such actions seem peripheral to the actual issue.

It actually reminds me of the story of Mulla Nasruddin, the Sufi sage, searching for his key under the lamp rather than where he had lost it. I feel the solution is out in the dark, but I'm searching under the street lamp because at least there is some light there. So I've started taking some steps into the dark.

One step is into exploring new rituals. We have been performing them by taking time on solstices and equinoxes to do rituals to reaffirm the depth of commitment and connection we feel with the earth.

I went to a workshop on Despair and Empowerment with Joanna Macy. The central despair ritual in that workshop involved people calling out the kinds of things that they saw happening in the world that led to despair, and then other people would call out, "I hear you. I hear you." Anyone who felt like weeping would go to a certain place and weep. People who were angry would beat pillows. Despair, anger, sadness gripped the whole room. It was a very moving experience which led to feelings of greater commitment and empowerment. During the feedback session at the end of the workshop, part of my criticism of the process was that ten million species are in danger, yet most of the people were calling out and reflecting on issues that were human-centered issues like famine, poverty, and abuse of children. Only a few were despairing about what was happening to animals, creatures, trees, and the earth itself.

Joanna came back to Bodhi Farm and we talked about constructing a nonanthropocentric despair ritual. We decided to call it the "Council of All Beings." Before the despair ritual, we identify with an animal, plant, or some feature of the landscape. Then we make masks to represent our ally or totem. During the ritual, we wear the masks; we represent the myriad species and we call out on their behalf. Participants have a very positive experience.

CT: Concerned women are encouraging all of us to be aware of the intuitive, caring, and loving factors in what we feel toward the welfare of the ecosystem. One of the bridges is a reexamination of the value of paganism. Through ritual and ceremony, we pay full respect and give full acknowledgement to nature. This fits in with what you are saying.

JS: I'm really interested in this process. From the "Council of All Beings" ritual, we also took another step which was a development of rebirthing therapy, which we called "Breath." In rebirthing, people use a connected breathing technique developed by Stan Grof to move into deeper layers of their own being to resolve personal problems. People are often moved to tears or anger through this therapy and also have profound insights about themselves and life. The "Breath" process adds another element to rebirthing, which is intention. Before each person begins, they decide on an intention for what they will work on during the session. Then they discuss this with the group leaders. It does seem that the experience one has during such a session is often related to the intention that one takes into the session.

We then began adding nonpersonal intentions, which developed into another ritual called "Eco-breath." Given that there is in reality no separation between person and planet, that any sense of alienation or isolation is illusory, we may use this breathing technique to tap into transpersonal and even trans-species awareness. This became a four-day workshop. People find a partner and each one takes it in turn to lie down and breathe, while the other cares for the breather. The kinds of intentions that we used were: "I intend to experience through my sadness the message from the rainforests and their response to our separation from them." Another intention was: "I intend to look at the way to heal and restore the antagonisms between women and men on the planet." So people's intentions were both personal and planetary.

CT: So here is a therapy working together with global awareness.

JS: Yes. These rituals have become a way of our tapping into the planet, to the creatures, the trees, and life forms. In this way the experience of the person is not separate from the rest of the planet. Through experiencing our own pain we may be tapping into the planet's pain, and through our pain we may thus contribute to the healing of the Earth.

CT: Are you feeling any disappointment with direct action?

JS: Direct action is good, but it isn't enough. The only justification I can see for it is to change people's minds. We might be able to damage Volkswagen's reputation so that they are forced to stop cattle ranching in the Amazon, and so protest does increase public awareness of the problem, but all it does is replace one cattle ranch company in the Amazon with another. Volkswagen will sell their interests and someone else will buy them. As far as the Amazon is concerned, nothing has changed, although people's awareness may have changed through that process.

CT: Are you saying there is no possibility of stopping the destruction of the Amazon?

JS: I'm saying there is no possibility other than through a tremendous change in people's understanding. There is no possibility of changing it by physically preventing something from taking place. None that I can see. Even if you can save this bit or that bit, the destruction that is taking place at the same time everywhere else is such that it is like tides coming in. You build a little wall on a certain patch of the beach and think you can keep the water out. But sooner or later the wall is going to go.

CT: Given your commitment to the rainforests, doesn't that leave you in a state of continual despair, frustration, and disappointment?

JS: No. It leads me to look for some direct ways to change the awareness of people, rather than through this indirect way of "Let's harass Volkswagen." We can explore fresh ways. There is no separation between myself and anybody else. It may be that the right person thinking the right thought is heard at a distance of 1000 miles. If we can get a clear enough shared intention, then we can affect things beyond ourselves. The week after the first "Council of All Beings" workshop, some whales were stranded on the coast nearby and people went to help rescue them. The local newspaper, *The Northern Star,* which is very conservative politically, had an editorial which was headlined, "Compassion for All Beings." Such a headline is totally out of character with *The Northern Star.* We couldn't help but wonder if the vibration around the place had changed and whether our work in the forest the previous weekend had somehow changed something.

CT: Are you saying that if *The Northern Star* can publish that sort of editorial, then there is hope?

JS: Yes, I think so. Again, I'm not at all certain that this kind of approach will work, but I feel desperate enough to try anything. I do feel that in the end people must understand that their self-interest cannot possibly be any different from the interests of the planet as a whole. Then we can find a way through this situation. People's sense of self has to expand beyond the shrunken social fiction of a self that we have inherited. It has to expand to a perception which really and truly believes in a shared biology.

Human Beings Are Conditioned

An interview with Jiddu Krishnamurti

Jiddu Krishnamurti was born May 11, 1895, at Madanapalle, 150 miles north of Madras, India. He was the eighth child in the family. His father, also named Jiddu, was employed by the British as a rent collector. One evening the boy was sitting on the beach with some other children when a theosophist named Charles Leadbeater picked him out to be the next World Teacher.

In January 1911, the Order of the Star was formed by leading theosophists and Krishnamurti was put at its head. He was sixteen years old. He stayed in England from 1912 to 1920, living with privileged families, learning and being exposed to Western culture. His brother Nitya accompanied him everywhere. In 1925, Nitya died, leaving Krishnamurti heartbroken and disillusioned for some time.

Sobered and strengthened by the experience, in July 1926 he began leading small camps. Three years later at the Star camp, in the presence of 3,000 Star members, Krishnamurti dissolved the order.

He began his talk that day with words that are familiar to those who have listened to him or read his books, "I maintain that Truth is a pathless land." He went on to say, "I do not want to belong to any organization of a spiritual kind . . . . You have been accustomed to being told how far you have advanced. How childish! Who but yourself can tell if you are incorruptible?"

That theme ran through every talk that Krishnamurti gave from the time he dissolved the order and resigned from the theosophists until the day he died. Throughout his long life he gave public talks around the world, lead camps, and initiated a number of small, progressively minded schools. A wide range of his talks and dialogues have been published and several videos are available.

I first began listening to Krishnamurti in 1968, when a friend in Sydney, Australia gained access to a number of his tape talks. I attended his talks several times in India, and I remember vividly how many of the people in his audience sat for hours though they were coughing horribly due to colds and chills, if not tuberculosis.

In 1982 and 1983, I had lunch with him a few times at Brockwood Park School in Hampshire. He began his meal by eating a single red apple which he first placed in the center of his plate, and afterwards a small serving of vegetable and salad. He asked me what I thought of India; "You can say anything you like. I'm not Indian, you know." I told him of the poverty, violence, and corruption I saw; I mentioned the beauty, the religious life, and the capacity of India to touch one deeply. He agreed. He told me that when he was a young man he had spent many years away from India. Upon his return, he was so saddened by what he saw that he spent his first week back in India in bed.

In October 1984, friends teaching at the school arranged for me to have an hour-long meeting with Krishnamurti, who was then in his eighty-ninth year. To say that this was a difficult interview would be to put it mildly. It seemed ironically fitting that part way through the meeting the tape recorder broke down, disrupting the conversation while the machine was fixed.

I had decided to explore the field of meditation with him. Frequently, he cut me off as I was talking. He was impatient in tone and continued to put forward his views quite abruptly. It was not that I disagreed with what he said, but his tone of speaking was hard to deal with. I'm sure he didn't want to speak as the final authority, but that, unfortunately, was the impression he gave. In a rather fatherly way, he would place his hand on top of mine from time to time—which admittedly softened the impact of being cut off in mid-sentence. With the end of his life approaching, I suspect that Krishnamurti was experiencing some frustration and disappointment about whether he had ever been understood in his own terms. So many of us who met with him over the years and listened to him speak were profoundly influenced by him. I wonder how much he realized this.

After meeting, he got up, we shook hands, and he walked briskly to the door. Then, almost as an afterthought, he turned to me, smiled, and said, "I hope we shall meet again." It was one of his last private interviews.

He continued to give public talks until his final talk in January 1986, in Madras, India, the area where he was discovered seventy-five years earlier. Krishnamurti told his audience that this might be his last talk, although hardly anybody realized what he was saying. He flew back to Ojai, California. He was dying. Two weeks later, just two days before his death, he asked to be taken outside in a chair. Once outside, he placed both hands together and bowed in all the directions to the beautiful nature surrounding him. He was ninety years old. After he died, his ashes were scattered in different parts of the world.

I am truly grateful that the interview took place. He was human, after all.

•

CT: I want to express my appreciation for the opportunity to meet with you today. I have looked forward to this for a long time. I would like to discuss and explore with you the field of meditation.

K: You are only concerned with meditation?

CT: One of the questions which arises with frequency is the question of meditation with form, structure, method, and technique as emphasized in many Eastern traditions. Your emphasis is that meditation must be free . . .

K: Right from the beginning, what do you mean by the world "meditation?"

CT: I make this concept interchangeable with such concepts as "observation," "mindfulness," "total attention." I use the word "meditation" in a broad way.

K: I'm asking what the word conveys, not the structure of meditation.

CT: What the actual word conveys?

K: The etymological meaning of the word.

CT: It means to give care and attention to the here and now.

K: We are not meeting each other. As I understand looking into the various dictionaries, it means "to ponder over," "to think over." The word in Sanskrit, I believe, means "to measure." It is merely a process of measurement.

CT: A measure of what?

K: What is, what should be, what one might achieve, what has been.

CT: And this comes within meditation itself?

K: We'll pry into the question "what is meditation?" not "how to meditate." We will not go into the various systems whether they be Buddhist, Hindu, Tibetan, or of any other guru who has a particular system of meditation. We are not discussing for the moment which is correct, but what meditation itself is.

The meaning of the word implies constant endeavor, constant self-recollectedness, constant observation of what one is doing, what one is not doing, attention to one's body, the movement of the body, the controlling of thought, and forcing thought to hold itself. All of this is implied in all of the systems, whether it is Zen Buddhism, or Tibetan, or even Christian contemplation. There is a sense of effort that is involved.

CT: The application of attention using effort is to give care and attention to thought.

K: All of that is implied. That is generally understood as meditation. I can include what you do in all of this. There is the whole Zen system, awareness, sitting up very still and having quieted the mind, controlling every reaction.

CT: I would say that the element of control certainly comes in because . . .

K: Of course, of course.

CT: But that is the *initial* expression due to the unfamiliarity of sitting still for varying periods of time.

K: So the central factor of meditation, yours, or others, is to control, in the sense of to hold.

CT: Yes, but that is a certain stage within the scope of . . .

K: That is measurement. That is why the word "meditation" implies "measurement," the beginning and the end.

CT: Isn't it quite often that the individual enters into a new area such as meditation and, given his or her conditioning, says, "I am going to meditate in order to come to somewhere else?"

K: Yes, generally, that is what is understood.

CT: That initial understanding of meditation may change as a person's understanding of meditation changes.

K: Yes, that is all measurement. "I do not understand, but I will understand. I am "this," whatever "this" is, and I will come to "that," which is a time interval." All that is an effort.

CT: Are you implying here that by establishing a measurement it in some way . . .

K: I'm observing, not condemning, agreeing, or changing. I'm clearly seeing that in meditation, those practicing meditation, taking various postures, cross-legged or whatever, there is the element of time, measurement, control, and something to be achieved. These are the central factors in all meditation.

CT: I get an underlying feeling that it is inappropriate . . .

K: I will tell you exactly that there is no underlying hidden something. There are the various factors of meditation which you and the others pursue. We never ask, "Why should I do all of this? Why should I meditate?" We do exactly the same thing in other directions. "I am a poor man and I want to become a rich man." "I don't know but I will know." "I am a clerk and I want to become an executive." "I don't know how to drive a car, but give me three weeks' time and I will learn it." It is the same movement.

CT: Yes, but there is a qualitative difference.

K: It is the same movement. You are trying to call something spiritual," right?

CT: Yes . . .

K: There—it is mundane. It is worldly. It is necessary. One asks for money, for shelter, therefore it is necessary. There is also a certain discipline there. Here too I must have discipline.

CT: But within . . .

K: I am not condemning anything. I am just watching.

CT: So you are pointing out that there are two major parallels between one movement of mind which is . . .

K: No parallel. They are exactly the same.

CT: They are exactly the same in terms of the movement of the mind.

K: The clerk says, "Give me another ten years and I will be manager." Here, too, "I am the beginner and I will come to the top," which is illumination. What is the difference between these two?

CT: I feel there is a certain difference. I don't wish to exaggerate the importance of the relativity of inner development.

K: It is exactly the same thing, only you call that "spiritual," "inner." This is psychological, subjective, under the skin; the other is done in a factory.

CT: I would think that the difference is that in spite of the identical nature of the two, one may contribute towards inner change and the other may deny it.

K: The other doesn't deny it. I have changed. I have a better house, a better garden. We have extended that same ambition to this so-called spiritual world.

CT: There is certainly an enormous danger in this transference from one kind of world into the other.

K: They are both the same. If I come to you and you tell me to meditate, I would reply that I don't know what you mean by that. You tell me to investigate, to pay attention to what I am doing. These are all things that you and others say. Right?

CT: Yes. Hopefully one communicates the actual position one is in at the present time.

K: What does that mean?

CT: That may mean that a person is experiencing frustration, confusion, or pain. It means that the primary emphasis . . .

K: Not primary or secondary. Let's look at what you are saying. I'm not criticizing you. I'm just observing what you are saying. Primary, the beginning. And with the beginning there is an end. That's what all of the gurus, all of the Eastern philosophers are saying: "Begin and you will get it. You will come near to it."

  Pursuing this logically, I can find a rationale for all of this. In the same way I have to live in this beastly society, so I must have more money, otherwise I would be destroyed. And one looks at that . . .

CT: And sees there is a certain emptiness to it.

K: That's it. Empty, right? Here if I do certain things, I won't be empty. I'm not criticizing anything. I will tell you what I think presently.

CT: As I listen to you what comes to mind is a condition of a number of people who find it extraordinarily difficult to make a leap which leaves behind their relative conditioning. What we have been describing is a material pursuit and a spiritual pursuit, which certainly implies a beginning but it may not imply an end.

> "That's the question. Is there within the human condition a part of an inward state where there is no conditioning— a small part?"

K: Forgive me, but you are repeating the same thing. That's what they all say, the Tibetan Buddhists, the Hindus, the gurus.

CT: Does the fact that something is repeated undermine it or disqualify it?

K: No, certainly not.

CT: By repeating I am trying to acknowledge the reality of those individuals' conditioning.

K: Human beings all over the world are conditioned as Christians, Buddhists, scientists, doctors, gurus. They are all conditioned by their culture. Those people who meditate and those who don't meditate are all conditioned by their culture.

CT: Is it a total form of conditioning, though?

K: That's the question. Is there within the human condition a part of an inward state where there is no conditioning—a small part? Is that what you are saying?

CT: Is there a small part that isn't conditioned? It does seem that given a certain outlook and attitude on life, we can look at mental processes clearly and directly, inwardly and outwardly. Therefore my question is: are there beneficial conditions for this kind of receptivity?

K: You'll have to reword your question, sir. What do you mean by "condition?"

CT: The bringing together . . .

K: I'm asking what do you mean by the word "condition?" The meditator is conditioned.

CT: Does the fact that the meditator is conditioned blind the meditator to a consciousness where one *can* see clearly?

K: That means he must be free of conditioning.

CT: At least not overwhelmed by it.

K: No. Isn't your question about the whole brain, which is after all, the only instrument we have? The brain is all the reactions, the responses, the neurological patterns, ambitions, greed, and envy. You are asking what is the conditioning that will help to free the brain of its conditioning. Are you sure you are asking that question?

CT: I think I'm conceited enough to think I know the answer. My question is: isn't there an element of mindfulness of observation within our brain which is able to see our mental processes clearly and directly?

K: So then we have to go into the question of observation, of seeing clearly. What do you mean by "seeing?"

CT: An awareness . . .

K: You see, I am not totally ignorant of your world. Don't put me into "awareness" and all that. What do you mean by "seeing," "observing?" I observe that sofa. The visual observation, the whole window, the color, what she [my daughter, Nshorna, playing on the floor] is doing. That is observation. The reactions are verbal: "bright," "dark," "black." So in that observation there is a verbalization of which one can also be aware. This is what is happening. "That is green." "That is a child." Remembrance and recognition. Then there is organization and representation. So these operate all the time, of course.

CT: Someone has an experience of seeing and they are affected by that experience.

K: Who is it that is being affected?

CT: In my use of language I would say that consciousness is affected by the field of mental experience. Moods, feelings, thoughts affect consciousness. One also identifies, for example, with "eye" consciousness in its connection with the field of vision. "I" see.

K: What is "consciousness?"

CT: The element of being conscious.

K: I am conscious of that chair.

CT: And in that there is a relationship formed between the element of consciousness . . .

K: So you would say that "consciousness" is its whole content. It is not just some content, including memories, reactions, fears, pleasure, pain, depression.

CT: But given our moment-to-moment existence, the content . . .

K: . . . changes, varies. But there is still content within this area which we call "consciousness." Whether small or big, that is not important. All of the physical, biological elements, reactions, responses, memories, tendencies, fear, sorrow, pain, depression, aspiration, envy, Britishness, "I am British," "I am Indian." All of that is in my consciousness.

CT: Right. In the form of language that you are using here, you are making the consciousness and the content totally identical.

K: The consciousness as we know it is nonexistent.

CT: Certainly one cannot have a separate existence from the other.

K: I didn't say the "other." You are saying the "other." I take an ordinary person; his consciousness is what he is, what he thinks, what he feels, what his aspiration is. He believes in God, he is a Catholic, non-Catholic, Protestant, Hindu, Buddhist. His own tendencies, his loneliness, his despair—all that is his consciousness.

CT: That is a condition of the consciousness.

K: This is *his* condition.

CT: Within the condition of the consciousness . . .

K: That is *his* consciousness. There is no other consciousness. You can invent another consciousness, superconsciousness, but you are still within consciousness.

CT: It is not a point which is clear to me because in looking, for example, at the chair, it is going too far to say the consciousness is the chair. The chair is an object in consciousness.

K: Of course.

CT: That object in consciousness means that there is a stated relationship which is there. Does that not apply equally to the whole scope of the mind experience?

K: So I'm seeing the whole brain as conditioned.

CT: Yes.

K: This conditioning, it is consciousness, right?

CT: Yes.

K: So if one is born in India one's consciousness contains all of the beliefs, superstitions, blah, blah, blah. If I'm born in a Roman Catholic family, it contains all the beliefs of Jesus, blah, blah, blah. This is conditioning. It is not one form of conditioning. They are both conditioned.

CT: I agree.

> "To teach that sublime thing, the brain must be tranquil. They say the same thing, the Buddhists, the Zen, the Hindu. The Christians haven't gone into this very deeply; the others have."

K: Now you come along and say, "Look, meditation is necessary to uncondition."

CT: Not necessarily to uncondition, but to find clarity with regard to the events that are happening.

K: That's very simple. Clarity of what is happening. In the meeting between political lead-ers, they are playing games. One is playing a political game to get elected and the other is definitely concerned about his opinions. You don't have to hear what they are going to say.

CT: No, it's quite apparent.

K: So we are moving away from the central fact that human beings are conditioned. They are programmed like computers. It is obvious. And human beings have been wanting and search-ing for something spiritual, what you call "religion." There have been people who have been saying, "Yes, there is some-thing there called spiritual, religious." It's been going on for a million years. Now you come around and say, "To find that, meditate," to put it crudely. I can put it more subtly if you want.

CT: I prefer subtlety.

K: All right. To teach that sublime thing, the brain must be tranquil. They say the same thing, the Buddhists, the Zen, the Hindu. The Christians haven't gone into this very deeply; the others have. Then the problem arises: Who is it that is going to make it silent? Who is the controller that controls thought? We never ask that question. We say that we must control thought.

CT: With inner observation . . .

K: "Inner Observation"—what do you mean by that?

CT: Meaning in this case sitting alone or . . .

K: Why should I do that when I can do it much more simply? In my relationship to my wife or husband, I watch my reactions there.

CT: But one doesn't exclude the other.

K: I begin there. I begin to see my relationship—the whole structure of myself. I don't have to ask you to teach me how to meditate.

CT: One certainly doesn't have to go . . .

K: That is what is happening in the world. You have become the guru. I am not being insulting, please.

CT: That is an insult.

K: So I would say, don't go through all this process of meditation and all of that. You have a very good opportunity to learn about yourself, know yourself, which is your relationship with nature, to your wife, to the politician, to your neighbor to whom you are talking. You can be aware of all of your reactions. Then go further. I don't need anybody to tell me how to go. That's my interest. I want to find out.

CT: Certainly that must be the major emphasis.

K: That is the only emphasis, not major.

CT: Okay, but given the . . .

K: Not okay. That is the only thing I can begin with because I'm related to everything in all my life.

CT: If I may say, people within the pressure of the social reality find it is . . .

K: . . . impossible.

CT: Exactly.

K: That means that you haven't understood society and your relationship to society. You have created this awful corrupt society because you are all like that.

CT: If the person is generally floundering within it, then . . .

K: Stop.

CT: Stop what?

K: This floundering. You see it is so simple. Someone sits up and says, "I'll help you." This game has been going on for a million years. Somebody, the priest, the psychiatrist, are all trying to help. Therefore you are making the listener who you are helping weak. Everything you find out. Don't depend on anybody.

CT: That is an indispensable emphasis—to encourage . . .

K: I don't want that. You see how you are using these words. I don't want to encourage anybody. I don't want to help anyone. I say, "Look, it is right in front of your nose, the whole world and yourself in relationship to the world. There is something much greater than that. Go into it." Why should I be a leader? Historically, how many leaders have we had?

CT: I am completely with you.

K: Sir, you talk about meditation. I say any form of conscious meditation is not meditation.

CT: That is tough language.

K: It is desire that is making me sit. It is desire that says I must achieve.

CT: Can't the desire . . . ?

K: You haven't come to what is desire. What is the nature of desire? Please, meditation is something entirely different, not all of this intellectual or emotional effort. This is something that must be *done*—not "must be done." Something which is consciousness with all of its travail, with all this anxiety, pain, loneliness. All that must be understood first. That's the corruption—not pornographic books and drugs. Corruption is when we are selfish, arrogant, envious. Begin there. Start there.

Joy Without Knowing

An interview with Sheila Cassidy

In the early 1970s, U.S. National Security Advisor Henry Kissinger and the CIA were directly involved in a ruthless campaign to destroy the democratically elected left wing government of Chile, headed by Salvador Allende. Following Allende's death in a military coup in October 1973, the secret police engaged in a nationwide hunt for Allende's supporters. Thousands were hunted down, tortured, and murdered.

During those years Sheila Cassidy was working in Chile in an emergency hospital and a shantytown clinic. One day friends asked her to treat a hunted man who had been shot by the secret police. Dr. Cassidy was arrested, tortured, and imprisoned for two months. In the face of fear and pain, her religious faith in God and humankind was challenged to the extreme. Amnesty International launched an international outcry against her treatment and that of countless others. She was expelled from Chile in December 1975. Dr. Cassidy spent the next eighteen months campaigning for the release of her fellow prisoners.

In 1977 she entered a convent to see whether she had a vocation. "After eighteen months I was asked to leave because I was ill and unhappy, so in July 1980 I returned to medicine."

Since 1982, Dr. Cassidy has been Medical Director of St. Luke's Hospice, Plymouth. In her book *Audacity to Believe*, she gives an account of her years in Chile. Her other books include *A Prayer for Pilgrims*, *Sharing the Darkness*, and *Good Friday People*. She is also a lecturer, preacher, and religious broadcaster.

What immediately struck me upon my arrival at St. Luke's Hospice was the cheerful atmosphere, indoors and outdoors. I had expected a silent place, rather like many old people's homes, but here there were children, dogs, and laughter.

Dr. Cassidy's office was littered with papers, notes, and books. "I am very untidy and disorganized because I'm always trying to cram something else into an overfull life."

Just before I left she gave me a poem which she had written. In part, it reads:

> I believe
> no pain is lost,
> no fear unmarked.
> No cry of anguish
> dies unheard,
> lost in the hail of gunfire
> or blanked out by the padded cell.
> I believe that
> pain and prayer
> are somehow saved,
> processed,
> stored,
> used in the Divine Economy.

Our meeting lasted about an hour. I appreciate immensely her willingness to talk openly and easily about her beliefs and the way her beliefs relate to her perceptions of others, including the dying.

•

CT: Who are the people that come here to die? What is the relationship of your religious experience to your work with those who are dying?

SC: We look after people who are terminally ill with malignant disease. They come in at any age, from twelve to one hundred. We often have people who are in their twenties and thirties, but most are between fifty and seventy. They come here primarily for pain and symptom control. For example, if the person has incurable cancer and is experiencing terrible pain, we give them a high priority. We also give high priority to someone who is very frightened. A lot of people come, are treated, and go home again. Others may come and stay here until they die, because they are especially vulnerable and needy. We give priority to the young. For example, we had a twenty-six-year-old woman who was here for two months, who died yesterday. She found it very hard to accept that she was dying and fought her illness to the very end, going to a party two days before she died.

CT: How do people find out about the hospice?

SC: Mostly they are referred by their general practitioners. St. Luke's Hospice is a medical institution, so they come through a medical referral.

CT: I assume that the hospice is not simply for Christians.

SC: The criteria for admission are purely physical and emotional needs and our ability to meet those needs.

CT: Are the staff of doctors and nurses expected to have religious beliefs?

SC: The staff must be competent in a clinical way. They must know what they are doing medically and nursing-wise. They must have the right type of personality. They have to be down to earth. We have no time for proselytizing Christians who like to shove religion down people's throats. Staff in a hospice must be loving and humor-filled people. This is a place of very basic caring. You have to be able to get your hands dirty and have a sense of humor.

CT: In your book *Sharing the Darkness* you mentioned that you were invited to give a public lecture called "The Spirituality of Caring." What does spirituality mean to you?

SC: Spirituality is a rather woolly term. Spirituality deals with our relationship with the unseen God and how we translate that relationship into our relationship with people.

CT: Is a relationship with the unseen God essential for a relationship here with those who are dying?

SC: I think the answer is no. The type of people who work here are nearly always people with some kind of faith. I suspect that people who have faith in an afterlife find it easier to spend time day by day with people who are dying. Having said that, we have one member of staff who does not believe in God. She is lovely because she believes passionately in people. We like our staff to have a deep faith, but we are wary of the person who wishes to convert the world to Jesus.

> "I do not mourn for the people I care for, although I am sad and distressed when they are distressed and afraid. I believe that when they die they are going on to something new and immeasurably wonderful . . . . "

CT: What does this sense of the unseen God and an afterlife provide for you in relationship to those who are dying?

SC: My belief in an unknown and transcendent God is absolutely fundamental to myself as a person and how I live my life. It provides my joy, my everything. My relationship with God is by far the most important thing in my life. It underpins the work that I do. In terms of my relationship to people, I suspect that my belief in God and an afterlife makes me very calm in the face of death. Of course, it's much easier to face another's death than one's own. I believe at a deep, gut level that death is not the end but the beginning. I do not mourn for the people I care for, although I am sad and distressed when they are distressed and afraid. I believe that when they die they are going on to something new and immeasurably wonderful, so how could I grieve for them, apart from being sad for their families and sometimes missing them myself?

CT: So your belief in an afterlife serves as a support for you in your work.

SC: Yes it does, but it also governs my attitude toward the people I care for. In a sense, what is often difficult for the dying is to be in contact with someone who is embarrassed to talk to them or is unable to talk about death. What we provide that is different from what most doctors and nurses provide is to be very comfortable with the dying.

CT: Are you saying that in a straightforward medical approach the primary consideration is the preservation of the patient's life? You have that consideration too, but you are facilitating a transition as well?

SC: My aim is to assist people to live their lives most fully day by day. I am concerned about the fullness of living rather than the length of days. My conversations with people would not necessarily be overtly spiritual. I would explore what people's beliefs are and what language they use before I got into any God talks.

CT: There is the transition from dying to death which we must face. We cannot say from an experiential standpoint, "I know what the afterlife is." So this is when faith begins. What is the origin of your faith here?

SC: I think that my faith in an afterlife is related to my faith in God in a way that I do not fully understand. I believe I have some kind of experience which is very difficult to pinpoint. It has nothing to do with book learning but only with my inner experience of God.

CT: The inner experience of God gives assurance to faith and to belief in an afterlife and something greater?

SC: It is a gamble. At an intellectual level I don't know, but I do believe.

CT: In your book there are many, many quotes from the Bible. The promise in the Bible of moving onto something greater after death is surely only for those who believe in God and, for a Christian, in Jesus too.

SC: I don't believe that. I believe that God *is*—whether we believe in Him or not. I don't believe at all that ultimate union with God is dependent upon our faith. I don't believe that Christians have a monopoly on it. I don't think I believe in hell at all.

CT: Isn't what you are saying a heresy?

SC: Is it? Jesus said that in His Father's house there are many mansions. Peter spoke of the net with many different people in it. I am certainly a very liberal Catholic. The conversations I have with my monastic friends do not make me think that I am totally outside the pale!

CT: What are some of the responses to dying that people go through?

SC: I speak a lot about emotional distress in terminal illness; about fear, loss, anger, alienation, and despair. The vast majority of people are scared. They experience fear of the unknown, fear of pain, and fear of disintegration. I think that is very natural. We have to elicit what people are afraid of and try to help them deal with these fears. But we can only be present for them in their existential fear of the unknown. We can take away a lot of fear, but not all of it.

CT: Each person has to cope with the unknown. Are you saying you can go so far with a person but no further?

SC: What I can do is be alongside the person when he or she is frightened. I can give you an analogy. I have to go to the Chilean Embassy. I have to witness with regard to somebody who was murdered in my presence. I have an existential fear of going near Chilean officials because I was imprisoned and done over by them. I have asked somebody from the Foreign Office to come with me. I know that he is not going to protect me, but he will accompany me in terms of this foolish fear. I am liberated enough to say: "I am scared, please come with me." In the same way, we accompany people here with their fears.

CT: Last week my eighty-four-year-old uncle died in a Blackpool hospital. I was with him in his last hours. It was clear to me how much he appreciated my presence as well as the presence of my aunt and my mother.

SC: To be with the dying is a ministry of presence.

CT: Do you think that a belief in God and in an afterlife have to go together? Since life is so vast and awesome, is it necessary to be concerned with something better later?

SC: The idea of a life after death makes sense to me because there are an awful lot of people who are unable to touch that which I touch and you touch. For example, the young woman who died yesterday had a hard life and a hard death. They are cheated people in some ways. It would be naive to imagine that everybody has a deep sense of peace and joy when they die. I was at a meeting this afternoon where we were talking about those who have died here in the last week. This young woman wanted to go on to get married and have children. In a sense, it comforts me that there is a beyond. If there is a God of eternity, who is a just and loving God, then I find it difficult to believe that some people are shortchanged forever. I like to think they will enjoy the fullness of living later. In direct answer to your question, I don't think that life after death has to go in with a belief in God, but I find it a very useful hypothesis! It works well for me.

CT: You said in your book that your contact with those who experience the incredible distress of suffering day in and day out reinforces your faith in a loving God. For some, this faith would seem to be emotionally and intellectually unbridgeable. How is it that your faith is strengthened rather than weakened?

SC: Some of those who experience great pain do also experience great depths of joy, but not all.

CT: What about those who only suffer and know no joy? Their life process has been a hard, painful struggle; the organism has been devastated by the circumstances of life and the person dies painfully right to the bitter end. How can that possibly reinforce faith in a loving God?

SC: I don't know that it does reinforce my faith. What reinforces my faith is when people do experience personal transformation, personal joy. Some years ago I entered a convent wanting to get closer to God. I failed. It didn't work for me. I was very unhappy and I left. Here in an ordinary, suburban city, I see such goodness from ordinary people. The father of the young woman who died came to the hospice today to pick up his daughter's remaining possessions and the death certificate. He came in his best suit. He was so grateful. I told him that he had been wonderful and so supportive. He said, "Well, I sat there with my daughter. Sometimes she would be horrible to me, but I knew she didn't mean it, so I just took it." There is such a selflessness in that. Selflessness is one of the holiest things. What reinforces my faith is the selflessness that can be elicited out of very ordinary people. I find that a very holy thing.

CT: It is truly beautiful that people are able to put aside their self-interest for others.

SC: I see so many people who are totally giving. One of the nice things about being here is that you meet people stripped of pretense, in the raw. Some of them are very selfish, but you also see so many people who are so lovely. I find that miraculous. I think the world is bloody marvelous and people are lovely. It is not that I don't know that people are wounded, fragile; but I believe they are fundamentally good.

CT: Your experience in Chile also certainly told you about the range of people's behavior.

SC: When a dying person feels loved and accepted, then the good things in that person begin to come out. We believe that the good is always there in the person even though they may seem initially very selfish.

CT: A loving social environment touches deep places within a person and brings out something profound.

SC: If there is time for it.

CT: A meaningful community endeavors to touch deep places of love, a deep well of goodness within each person. But isn't it possible that this human love is then projected onto a larger dimension called God?

SC: Perhaps the God language provides a language for that which *is*. Christian scriptures provide for me a language for my experience. What I experience which the nonbeliever doesn't is a personal sense of a relationship with God.

CT: The Christian God is a very personalized form of God. How vital is this God to people, to the dying?

SC: I don't think it is vital at all. One of our staff has no sense of a personal God and she is probably rather more loving and more selfless than I am. I would interpret that as showing that God works in mysterious ways. It's the language, isn't it?

CT: In a way then, the God language isn't so vital.

SC: I have seen people who are equally selfless who are professed believers or professed atheists. I spent a lot of time with Marxists who didn't have a faith. I don't feel any need to convert those who have no faith. In a sense, though, I do think nonbelievers are missing out on a certain dimension of joy.

CT: Jesus said that you shall know them by their fruits.

SC: Yes, exactly.

CT: In a way your Christianity is equally a non-Christianity, isn't it?

SC: I am theocentric rather th in Christocentric in my worship. I worship the unseen face of God. I quote a lot from the Old Testament. I am equally turned on by the different scriptures. What makes me want to lie on my face in the dark is talk of the unseen transcendent God. I used to say that if somebody discovered that Jesus was not true, I would barely bat an eyelid, but that is not quite as true as it was awhile ago. I have been looking a lot lately at the risen Christ and that has become meaningful for me. But what gets me in my religious guts is the sense of the unseen God. That is the God before whom I prostrate myself.

CT: You come across as closer to the mystical traditions of God rather than to the conventional belief in God the Father and God the Son.

SC: That's true. My belief is deeply rooted in the Christian mystical

> "We offer a professional loving which recognizes that people are precious whether they are demented or disfigured or behave badly. They are precious quite simply because they are people."

tradition. I am turned on by the mystics. My experience of God gives me a joy beyond all knowing.

CT: Given your sensibilities and awareness to God, and given the application and the skillfulness of the language which is appropriate to yourself and to those who are dying, do those who are dying change their views very much about life after spending time in a hospice like this?

SC: Some people change a lot. We had a lady recently who came to us frightened, angry, and believing she was allergic to the painkillers. She was also resentful of the institution. Over a period of about a month she did a total somersault. She lay there and kept saying to us, "It sounds crazy but I have never been so happy. I have never known such love exists. I am totally at peace." She actually came back to her religion, not in a very deep sort of way. She was a lapsed Catholic. She was remarkably at peace. We see that happens for the dying from time to time. It happens enough for us to be very familiar with this kind of change. If people are here long enough, it happens often. I think people are amazed at the love they receive. What we offer to people is a nonjudgmental relationship. We accept people where they are. If they come with delinquent children and a mistress, we don't bat an eyelid. We offer a professional loving which recognizes that people are precious whether they are demented or disfigured or behave badly. They are precious quite simply because they are people.

CT: You have the support of God, the support of the social environment, and you deal with probably the most difficult period of a person's life, that is their impending death. Amidst all of this, is there anything which you regard for yourself as being acutely difficult to acknowledge?

SC: Yes. I don't spend as much time with the patients as I used to. When I began about 10 years ago I was the only doctor and I was very close to a lot of people. Now I have a number of different staff. I am heavily engaged in lecturing and I am conscious that I am not as close to them as I used to be.

CT: I can't help noticing the mass of paperwork in your office. Are you bogged down in administration?

SC: It's not so much administration as correspondence about all sorts of things. Sometimes I feel as if I am drowning in paperwork! If I'm rational about my sense of guilt, I would say it is inevitable in my role. I think I run a lovely ship. What I am experiencing is part of the pain of distancing myself because I am at the head of the hospice. The other staff here get both the work and the joy. I am sufficiently close to enough people to know how much I love working with people. Sometimes I have a bit of weariness with the work.

CT: What aspect of the work do you feel some weariness over?

SC: It is a weariness in having close, deep conversations. There is no doubt that one-to-one conversations with dying people are wonderful but draining. Sometimes if I am tired I will step back from it. Quite often I am here until seven or eight P.M. I could be using the time to get close to people. It is not so necessary, because others here are doing that. But I don't do it to get on with the paperwork. I am conscious of a degree of distancing.

CT: What gives you renewal when you are weary? You said that you have just written another book. That could be considered an extension of paperwork.

SC: Oh, all sorts of things renew me—television, shopping, especially for clothes, picnics down the river, going for walks, having friends for dinner. The creative side of my nature is very important to me—writing, preparing broadcasts, sewing, playing with my house. I really love the writing, the playing with words and ideas. Prayer and going away on retreat renew me, though in a different sort of way. Retreats can be hard.

CT: In your daily life, how much inspiration do you get from the Bible?

SC: What is most important is my relationship with God. The scriptural texts are all part of that. The central thing has to do with the love of God. I suppose that one can experience God in very beautiful surroundings, such as when listening to beautiful music or watching a sunset, but you can also experience His presence in very ordinary surroundings. I went to London last week to give a lecture and I sat in an empty tube train. I had a tremendous sense of the presence of God, of loving Him and being loved. I felt quite overwhelmed, though at the same time quite aware of where I was.

    I value that kind of experience more than those which come in a more romantic setting. If I experience God when I'm desperate with insomnia or crying or in the tube or car, it seems a more stripped sort of encounter than in the middle of a sunset or a beautiful liturgy. I think that's why I would pray by choice in the dark or in an empty room.

CT: "Blessed are the poor in spirit for theirs is the Kingdom of God" is the first of the beatitudes of Jesus.

SC: Yes. Words like "dazzling dark" make me want to lie on the floor and pray. Sometimes I am scared that I kid myself. I don't spend an hour praying every morning. I think if I were really spiritual I would spend an hour every morning and every night praying. In practice, maybe I spend half an hour or twenty minutes. It doesn't feel enough, but I can't cope with any more at the moment. I can cope with more when I am on holiday. Sometimes I worry about that and sometimes I don't.

CT: Do you pray with words?

SC: No. I don't pray with words. I pray by sitting and opening up myself to God. It is just sitting there. I haven't prayed with words for years and years. I have never been desperately into saying prayers. There is, though, a certain spiritual pride which comes through praying without words. So I think it is good for me to be able to pray with words also—but the only sort of words I seem to use are "Help!" or, more often, "I love You."

We Used Hammers

An Interview With Jim Perkins

And they shall beat their swords into plowshares
and their spears into pruning hooks;
Nation shall not lift up sword against nation,
Neither shall they learn war anymore.

Isaiah 2:4

The movement for peace and justice has an ebb and flow in terms of public interest. Some of the peace demonstrations in the 1980s in the West were among the largest such gatherings ever witnessed, with hundreds of thousands turning out to put pressure on the superpowers to disarm. Membership and activity tend to be influenced by the degree of publicity an event gets. What is often forgotten is that the issues facing people and planet do not go away. This means that a small core of activists keep the flame of protest alive during the weeks, months, and sometimes years when the media perceives that there is nothing newsworthy going on in the movement.

One of those who keeps the flame of protest alive is Jim Perkins. I first met Jim in 1978 when he came to participate in a retreat in New England. He gave me an enormous jar of pure maple syrup to bring back to old England.

Jim was born in 1938. From 1961 to 1968, he taught social studies in high school and participated in the civil rights struggle as a Freedom School Teacher in Mississippi. In 1968 he founded and directed the Manhattan Country School Farm, which offered family farming and environmental skills and values to inner city children.

In recent years, Jim has participated in a number of insight meditation retreats. He also spent six months practicing prayer and meditation at the Doshingi Monastery, Mount Tremper, New York, before becoming part of a war resistance community in Maryland.

Although he is not a Christian, Jim has taken to heart the Biblical prophecy, "they shall beat their swords into plowshares." At the time of this writing in 1989, more than seventy people had participated in twenty-four Plowshare actions, which involve breaking into nuclear weapons bases, disarming parts of the weapons, and pouring blood on them.

The judiciary has come down heavily on these peace activists. Sentences have ranged from six months up to staggering twelve- and eighteen-year sentences for what is basically the destruction of government property and criminal trespass. The media have paid very little attention to these actions, even when one of the cases involved a mother who was sentenced to eighteen years for her nonviolent direct action.

Despite the imposition of severe sentences, peace activists with religious convictions keep coming forward to engage in such actions. As one sympathizer pointed out, "It reveals the lengths that the government is willing to go to prosecute and jail nonviolent people who resist nuclear war and interventionist policies. It is ironic that those responsible for crimes in the Iran-Contra affair receive immunity while peace activists receive long imprisonment for having acted in obedience to their understanding of divine and international law."

Jim is now executive director of the Traprock Peace Center in Deerfield, Massachusetts and a member of the national council of Fellowship of Reconciliation, the renowned religious organization for peace and social justice. He is also a contractor and carpenter. He has five children.

The interview took place during a Buddhist retreat about half-way through Jim's prison term. He was granted religious furlough for the weekend in order to participate. He kindly agreed to allow other participants to listen in while he talked about his action at the nuclear weapons base.

Ploughshare activists continue to engage in numerous actions throughout the U.S.A. In December 1991, Ploughshare activists climbed the fence and poured blood on the White House. They appeared in court in February 1992 for defacing the huge statue of Columbus fronting Union Station in Washington. They used blood and spray paint for "500 years of genocide." Despite heavy fines and prison sentences for various actions, the campaigns continue. Men and women, mostly committed Christians, continue to offer themselves for protest against war and injustice. Ploughshare activists regularly participate in "Faith and Resistance Spiritual Retreats."

•

JP: I want to start with some words of appreciation. It's not at all like prison here! In prison, there is a background of grumbling and complaining. The food isn't anything like it is in prison. It's wonderful to be with you. I wish I could be here longer.

CT: Jim, I would like to discuss your personal involvement in the peace movement and I'd like to begin with the break-in at the nuclear weapons base in Orlando, Florida, in December 1983. What were the events that led up to this period when you and other men and women first committed yourselves to this peace action?

JP: In December 1983, NATO began to deploy Pershing II missiles in Europe. That was an evident shift in what the United States said it was doing; a shift from a nuclear policy of deterrence to one of first strike. That is attack theory. These are attack weapons and it seemed to me important to point that out to the public and not let it go by as a secret.

CT: What steps did you take personally? Who did you get in contact with?

JP: I had been involved in various kinds of social action since the early 1960s. I was campaigning for civil rights and I was involved in the anti-Vietnam War movement. I never did anything that got me into prison. This road to prison really started with a retreat that I went to with Daniel Berrigan. It became very clear to me that to be with Daniel meant I couldn't play around. I walked out of the retreat center onto the highway not knowing whether I was going this way or that way, it was that disorienting. What I finally did was, I went this-a-way—to live in the community where Daniel Berrigan's brother was living. It's in Baltimore, called Jonah House.

CT: For several years you have been coming here to the Insight Meditation Society, practicing Buddhist meditation. How did you fit into a Christian community and the peace work there?

JP: I fit in very well and felt very comfortable with them. In fact, I thought that I was really seeing Christianity for the first time. They seemed to be very comfortable with me, some more than others. The more I kept my mouth closed, the more comfortable it was. When I went to Jonah House I already pretty much knew what I was getting into; that was part of the decision. Both Philip and Daniel Berrigan were part of the first Plowshares action in 1980. They have been a guiding force in this movement since that time.

CT: So you went to the base four months later. What took place in the period between December 1983 and Easter Sunday 1984, when you entered the missile site?

JP: There were eight of us that managed to get together. We were members of the Atlantic Life Community, which is a series of communities involved in peace actions up and down the Atlantic coast. We got to know each other through peace actions at the Pentagon and other places. Soon after that, we started spending weekends with each other, exploring possibilities of engaging in a direct action together. We would find a church to spend the weekend in, bring a lot of food, and spend two or three days talking about the proposed action, talking about our feelings, our convictions, our doubts and fears. We were trying to see what this would mean for us on a personal level, as well as trying to build up a degree of trust between ourselves.

CT: After that you decided to go to Orlando?

JP: We met about every other weekend for four months. We only decided where we were going to go and what we were going to do at the very end of this period. We decided we wanted to focus our action on the Pershing II missile because that was the missile of the moment, as far as NATO deployments were concerned. The Pershing was made in Orlando, so that is why we went there. Some of us hitchhiked. Two of us took a plane and the others carpooled. When we arrived in Orlando, there were people who very generously helped us in faith, even though it was a great risk for them to do so.

CT: Then came Easter Sunday, which was on April 22. Coincidentally, it happened to be my fortieth birthday. I regard your action, by the way, as the best possible birthday present. So, on Easter Sunday, what took place?

JP: In the early hours after midnight, we had a short period of silence together in the house. Then we got into two cars and went to the Martin Marietta nuclear weapons base. We were carrying a bolt cutter, hammers, crowbars, bottles of blood, and documents. We quietly unloaded them out of the cars and went through the woods along a path we had scoped out on another day. We then hid ourselves in the bushes near the back of a building that was called the Pershing Missile Kit Building. We didn't have any inside contacts at the Martin Marietta plant. All we knew was that there was this building called the Pershing Missile Kit Building. It sounded like that would be where they were shipping those things out of. So we hid out there for about an hour while the mosquitoes and the chiggers did their number on us. We watched for guards and didn't see any.

It was about four in the morning. Then we crept up to the fence, applied the bolt cutter, and entered the base. We broke into two groups. One of us pried the door open in the Pershing Kit Building and went inside. One of these kits, which was in a huge box, was used to convert Pershing I missiles into Pershing II missiles. We chose one of about forty boxes and opened it, took parts out and began to destroy them, We hung a banner in the building saying, "Violence ends where love begins." We hung pictures of children and loved ones around.

The other group went to some Pershing II launchers, which are like huge trucks. They climbed onto one of the launchers and cut the hydraulic and electrical cables. In a yard full of these launchers, they chose one, made it so that it couldn't be used, put a banner on it, and poured blood on it.

> "We had to ask ourselves how would we feel if just one of our number was wounded or killed. What would the effect be on the person who did the deed? Would it have all been worth the risk? "

Then we all came back to a very obvious spot in front of the Pershing Kit Building, sat in a circle on top of some pallets, and waited to be discovered.

CT: Given all the paranoia with regard to terrorists, your lives must have been very much at risk. You could have all been shot at any time while inside this missile factory. How were you working with all that fear?

JP: Yeah, fear, and also wondering whether this was a very smart thing to be doing! [Laughter] We had to ask ourselves how would we feel if just one of our number was wounded or killed. What would the effect be on the person who did the deed? Would it have all been worth the risk? When the guards came, we were all holding hands in a circle and we began singing, "Peace is flowing like a river."

CT: What was the response of the guards? They saw you sitting there as a group in the middle of the night singing and their missiles having been hammered.

JP: The first person who might have seen us was driving by in a car, quite close by. He almost came over to us and then sped off. We didn't see anything more for about fifteen minutes. The second guard that came up was a woman, an Israeli woman, and her reaction when she saw us was to say, "My God, what are you doing here?" She had sincere wonder in her voice, not so much concern or fear. She stayed nearby. She left her gun in her holster and got on her car radio and called for reinforcements. They began to arrive in great numbers from many different police agencies.

They left us there for another two or three hours while they checked out the scene. The Martin Marietta executives came and looked over the mess. We were taken away from the group one by one and questioned, all very politely, remarkably politely, and then they let us go back onto our pallet to sit down in our circle. About another three hours later, we were arrested and taken to the Orange County jail. This was a nasty place. The cell that I was in for a month before the trial was ten by fourteen feet. There were eight men in this cell and we only got out for an hour a day to eat. There was no exercise period. There was no sorting of criminals. There were people in the cell on traffic violations and there were rapists.

CT: Were you handcuffed?

JP: Yes. After we were finally arrested there was all of that heavy steel kind of stuff. That lasted from then until the time we got to Danbury Prison in September.

We had a lot of legal points we wanted to make at the trial and we weren't able to say very many of them. We wanted to make the argument that these weapons were illegal. We brought an indictment of the Martin Marietta Corporation and the U.S. Government into the action with us, making the point that these weapons have no right to exist by law.

CT: By whose law?

JP: By international law and also by Judeo-Christian law. The trial lasted six days. We were going to make the argument that we have a human right to act against these weapons because these weapons endanger life. It's a legal principle analogous to breaking into a burning house to rescue the children that are on the second story. There are various legal standards that you have to meet to make this argument. We worked hard to meet them, but we didn't get a chance. We were not allowed to bring in expert witnesses, including lawyers, historians, and biologists who would testify as to the imminent danger of nuclear weapons.

CT: What were you actually charged with?

JP: We were charged with conspiracy and destruction of U.S. Government property. The jury took about an hour to eat lunch and find us guilty. We were all given the same sentence by the judge—three years.

CT: That seems like a very tough sentence! In Europe, there have been break-ins at nuclear bases, such as when the women broke in at Greenham Common. They have generally been given seven or fourteen days in prison. In West Germany, there was a fine and no prison sentence when peace activists were arrested after cutting through the fence.

JP: Yes, and there have been harder ones. Ours was the eighth in the series of Plowshare actions. The ninth of the series happened in Minneapolis at the Sperry Rand Company. Two people went in and smashed a prototype computer that was being built as part of a missile guidance system. These people were tried and convicted and given a six months suspended sentence by the judge. He gave a very interesting opinion. He said there is some kind of strange double standard going on here. The judge had just previously heard a case where Sperry Rand had been taken to court by the government for a three million dollar overcharge on one contract. The government had asked that the Sperry Rand Company pay back ten percent of that money to the government, who hadn't sought any prosecution for any of the executives. So the judge was wondering what was going on here, because the U.S. attorney wanted to throw these two young peace activists away [imprison them].

CT: What has happened at other Plowshare actions?

JP: The tenth in the series was in Providence, Rhode Island. People went into the Electric Boat Shipyard and hammered on D-5 missile tubes. This D-5 missile system will be going into the new Trident submarines. It's going to transform these weapons from retaliatory weapons into first-strike weapons. These weapons are going to be extremely accurate.

The eleventh break-in was at a Minuteman missile silo in Kansas by four people: Helen Woodson, who, incidentally adopted ten children with Down's Syndrome, Carl and Paul Kabat, brothers who are also priests, and an American Indian named White Feather. Carl spent a lot of time doing work among the poor in Peru and Chile, and his brother worked in American cities. The four of them walked one night through the cornfields pulling a ninety-pound jackhammer and air compressor, broke through the fence, and went to work on the lid of this missile silo.

They were tried and convicted. Helen and Carl were given *eighteen-year sentences.* Paul was given a ten-year sentence and White Feather was given an eight-year sentence, for this protest which did a total of $11,000 damage.

CT: That seems to me a savage and barbaric sentence. Why isn't there a great deal of publicity about it? Four people committed no violence to anybody and did a trivial amount of damage to U.S. government property. Why is there no public outcry?

JP: It's not for lack of people trying to get it publicized. It did receive a little publicity in a Kansas City newspaper. This is the pattern of the way these actions get publicized. The first one, the Plowshares Eight, which involved Daniel and Philip Berrigan, did get some nationwide publicity. The other actions have had local publicity only. News items go out on the AP wire and UPI wire. Sometimes the hometown paper will pick up the story. The *New York Times* said nothing about the action out in Kansas, or the trial, or the sentence. The trial lasted for four days.

CT: Are the actions likely to continue considering quite a number of you are already in prison? Has the shock of this eighteen-year sentence frightened other peace activists?

JP: I don't really know. The twelfth of these actions happened during the Kansas trial, in Kansas, when a man from Vermont, who was acting alone, hammered a Minuteman missile silo. Clearly, the authorities are trying to deter these actions. They have decided that this has to stop. We have every reason to believe that the Justice Department does speak to the prosecutors and to the judges and there does seem to be a kind of national policy on how to deal with these actions. I think this last sentencing shows the heavy hand of Edwin Meese [Attorney General under President Ronald Reagan]. Whether it will work or not, we will have to wait and see.

CT: Are you in prison with any of the others with whom you engaged in the action?

JP: There are four of us in the Danbury Prison Camp, two from the Griffiths Plowshares—the action that immediately preceded ours at a Strategic Air Command base in Rome, New York. These people went into a hangar and hammered on a B-52 bomber that was being converted to carry air-launch cruise missiles. One of the people who engaged in that action was Elizabeth McAllister, one of the members of my community, along with Phil Berrigan's wife. She is in the Alderson Prison in West Virginia now on a three-year sentence. Two of the men from that action are in Danbury Prison, plus Todd

Kaplan, my codefendant, and me. A fifth member of our group, Per Herngren, a Swedish national, is in heavy security because he is a foreigner.

CT: Are there any others in prison through heavy-handed treatment by the government?

JP: C.W. Deaton. He's a Texan and born-again Christian. He's imprisoned with us at Danbury. He's serving a fifty-year sentence. Yes, fifty years, for defying the Russian grain embargo. This embargo was a bad idea anyway. He's hoping to get pardoned one day. So far he's served nine years of his sentence.

CT: The peace movement tends to flow in waves of energy and enthusiasm and then it reaches a trough. In your time in prison, have you given much thought to new ways of expressing protest? And how can those of us who are not in prison contribute to the peace movement?

JP: We are interested in civil disobedience. We think it is very important to say "No!" in a very strong way to the politicians and the nuclear armament industry. Christian people tend to say "Not in My Name." For me, "Not in My Name" means not in the name of humanity.

CT: In prison, are there any restrictions on your expression? Can you have letters going out or coming in?

JP: There are restrictions on books. They can do what they want with our mail, but the mail comes and goes very easily, as far as I can see. Nothing that I've sent out has been censored. All the incoming mail is opened, but I don't know if it is really read.

CT: Where does much of your mail go?

JP: A lot of it goes to Florida. "Swords Into Plowshares" is our slogan. We say the sword is the Pershing missile and the plowshare is the peace community in Florida. When we look for results, that's what we look for. We did leave an invigorated peace community in Florida.

CT: Some Christians view the missiles as an idol.

JP: American nuclear policy is a state religion. These weapons are modern idols. It is up to us to smash them. One of the arguments that we are trying to get into court is that we can't live with American nuclear policy and at the same time claim to have any right to practice our religion.

CT: Is the argument that these missiles deny true religious feelings and expression being heard by the courts?

> "Nuclear missiles are clearly illegal under international law and under the Nuremberg principles. As individuals, we have the right and responsibility to act against our government when it is acting illegally. We want this argument heard in court."

JP: Liz McAllister began to work on it for the Griffiths trial and a refinement was brought to the Second Circuit Court of Appeals in New York. One of our friends is Ramsey Clark, who was the Attorney General under Johnson. He's taken part in many noble causes and has a great deal of hope for this argument. He thinks that over the years this will be the important legal argument.

Nuclear missiles are clearly illegal under international law and under the Nuremberg principles. As individuals, we have the right and responsibility to act against our government when it is acting illegally. We want this argument heard in court. So far the judges have said, "We're not going to hear that argument." But the judge in Syracuse said, "That's an interesting argument. Someday some judge is going to hear it, but it's not going to be me."

CT: The government may have to start listening to the various forms of sustained protest taking place via the courts. Presumably that is part of the motive of those who engaged in such peace actions.

JP: It's a tough issue for the peace movement. Some people believe in the courts and some don't. When we get together in our communities, the communities will almost always break down into those who want to do a sophisticated legal defense and those who think that the courts are hopeless and would simply like to speak the truth, forgetting about legal form. Our friends in Kansas City who got eighteen-year terms were among those who thought you can't talk to these people in their language. They just spoke the truth as they saw it in a very powerful and eloquent way. But they did not follow legal form, which, by the way, makes it very difficult for them to appeal.

CT: Have they decided to appeal? I know that Helen, who has the eighteen-year sentence, wrote to you. What is she experiencing at this time?

JP: She's being held under harsh circumstances, but nevertheless is experiencing joy and community. There was no precedent for the eighteen-year term. However, she has made no compromises with the prison authorities and has denied all offers to help her receive clemency. In her view, the monstrosity of nuclear weapons dwarfs the injustice to her, and they are the issue. She doesn't want anyone to make *her* the issue. "Don't worry about me," she writes, "abolish the weapons."

CT: In other words, she has chosen to keep her faith; not to have faith in the legal system. In what ways is she being supported?

JP: We have a Peace Prisoners' Fast on the first day of every month in the various prisons around the country. All of us who were involved in these actions fast. We ask other people who are interested to join with us. Also, there is a woman who takes our writings and sends them out to the local peace newsletters and the local groups around the country. Each one of our groups has a support committee which publishers a newsletter and sends money for the prisoners' commissary funds, if necessary, or to help out their families.

CT: I would like to express my deep appreciation to you for your concern, your courage, and to all those who are saying "No!" in such a clear and direct way. May these contributions to peace and justice make inroads into the minds of people in government.

One more question: how are your five children handling their dad being in prison?

JP: They think it's great!

The Crisis Is Here Now

An interview with Jonathon Porritt

Jonathon Porritt comes from a privileged background. He is one of the seven percent of British children who go to private instead of state schools. He went to Eton and from there to Oxford University, where he obtained a degree in Modern Languages.

When he was eighteen years old, his parents bought land in New Zealand, which had the name Rangitopuni. Jonathon went there to plant pine trees on the land in well-ordered rows. It was through this experience that he developed a deep relationship with the environment. Nearby was a five-acre patch of land which somehow escaped the attention of the developers. This was called "The Cathedral," because the native trees soared up like the nave of a cathedral; below, it was hushed. There, Jonathon says, "Songs of praise were uttered." He says, "I have learned that wildness abounds far beyond the ever-shrinking confines of wilderness. There is wildness in your own backyard, in your garden or somewhere down your favorite walk, even in your windowbox, but only if there is wildness in your soul."

During years of teaching in a school in West London, he became increasingly interested in the fledgling Ecology Party, as it was then called. His presence in the party was quickly felt. He became an articulate campaigner on Green issues and within a few years was one of the chairpersons.

Generally speaking, the kind of educational upbringing and background that Jonathon had is regarded as being more suitable for conventional politics or industry, commerce, or the civil service, but he chose none of those areas. As an Ecology

Party candidate, he ran on seven occasions in local, general, and European elections. In September of 1984 he published *Seeing Green,* a book which provides the general reader with a clear explanation of the politics of ecology. Following the book's widespread success, he made many appearances on television, radio, and in numerous public forums, which established him as a leading spokesperson for the Green movement. He gave up teaching to concentrate full-time on ecological issues and was appointed director of Friends of the Earth. He retired from this position in 1989. In 1992 he attended the world conference on the environment in Rio de Janeiro.

In 1991, Jonathan put out the book *Save the Earth,* with a foreword by Prince Charles. His series of six documentaries entitled "Saving the Earth" appeared on British television in 1992.

Jonathan has one daughter. Now based in London, he can be seen pedaling his way around town, one of Britain's most respected environmentalists. He acknowledges that his life, like that of other committed people, leaves little time for aloneness and reflection, which he admits "matters enormously." He was once giving a public talk at Sharpham House in Ashprington, a community close to where I live. Prior to the talk there was a forty-five minute silent meditation and afterwards Jonathon told the audience that it was the first time in four or five months that he had had the opportunity to experience that quality of silence.

The interview with Jonathon took place in his office at the time, a small room on the top of the Friends of the Earth's building in London. We explored some of the moral and ethical principles facing the politics of ecology today.

•

CT: In the very last passage of *Seeing Green,* you say, "Stripped of a spiritual dimension, politics in today's world is a hollow shell, and religion stripped of its political dimension is irresponsibly escapist." What do you mean by "spiritual"?

JP: I suspect that I kept the definition as loose and open as possible because one of the central principles of Green thinking is the acknowledgement and recognition of diversity. If you start to define things too closely, you start to exclude people by virtue of the narrowness of the terms that you are relying on. It has also been part of my understanding not to narrow down that concept to any one interpretation. But that approach can be criticized because of a lack of intellectual rigor, or, indeed, a lack of spiritual integrity, if you are not prepared to specify what you mean by the word. To me, the word has a meaning that is quite clear. I have always used it to refer to that aspect of human nature that allows people to transcend the limitations of their material world, to seek meaning in that which cannot be defined materialistically or scientifically.

CT: There *is* the need to transcend materialistic ambitions through concern for the planet. On the other hand, all too often there can be neglect of the quality of one's life.

JP: Yes, though I doubt that's true of most people in Green organizations today. I believe that people think very carefully about the quality of their life. They think carefully about what they eat, how they travel, the clothes they wear; whether they are wasting things; whether they are dealing with people the way they should be; are they becoming victims of a consumer society? However, it would not necessarily be true to say that such a lifestyle concern always embraces a spiritual dimension. People aren't necessarily thinking day-to-day about what it is that makes life good and what keeps us from trespassing too heavily on the planet. But I have been impressed over the years by a significant proportion of people in the Green movement that do feel a spiritual dimension in their lives as well as the quality of life dimension. Unless our way of life actually does reflect our political beliefs and our philosophical position, then it's barely worth putting those beliefs and that position down on paper. Everything we do impinges directly on the lifestyle and quality of life of people in this country and in other countries.

But for me that would not wholly define the spiritual dimension. There are many people in the Green movement who would show this concern for the quality of life and yet who would dismiss as irrelevant any further thoughts about what the spirit is that underlies their decision, actions, and ethics. They would quite clearly distinguish between an ethical position and a spiritual one.

CT: What kind of criterion is at work to say this is an ethical or a spiritual position?

JP: Spiritual would include ethical, but ethical doesn't necessarily include the spiritual. Ethically, for instance, people in the Green movement would say it is not acceptable to go on using the Earth's resources in such a way as to deny two-thirds of humanity the right to exist with any dignity or decency. If this is your position, then the moral consequence is that you have changed your lifestyle accordingly to accommodate that moral principle. But they wouldn't necessarily link that to any spiritual attitude or any other religious or metaphysical concerns. It would be wrong to say that everybody in the Green movement is concerned about the spiritual dimension. But there are a large number who are concerned.

> "... there is a real ethical dilemma as to whether we look upon humankind as being a part of creation—a biocentric view—or whether we see humankind as separate from the rest of creation."

It's a question, I think, of taking those moral, ethical, and ecological principles and seeing whether one finds something that embraces them all in a different and deeper way. To me, for instance, one must acknowledge the truly radical meaning of that very simple phrase—to live in harmony with the Earth—and make that possible and feasible. I actually think that you need a spiritual relationship with the Earth. I do not think it is possible to achieve such harmony in a purely utilitarian, functional way.

CT: Are you equating the utilitarian aspect with voluntary simplicity?

JP: Well, not necessarily. Because again, there are people who follow the principles of voluntary simplicity who would do so to uphold the quality of life for as many people as possible, but not necessarily for any deeper spiritual concerns. To take a classic divide within the Green movement, there is a real ethical dilemma as to whether we look upon humankind as being a part of creation—a biocentric view—or whether we see humankind as separate from the rest of creation. The latter position has dominated the development of society and civilization for the last four or five hundred years and has led to what I consider to be almost an entirely anthropocentric view of life. The former position was certainly held predominantly by what are referred to as "primitive people," who are in the web of life rather than apart from it. Now, for me, the anthropocentric vision of man—and I mean "man" rather than "human"!—is of a dominant dominion rather than a caring, responsible stewardship. A biocentric view of life needs to be interpreted in a more spiritual way.

CT: In many respects, our Western society has created a separation from the planet through a massive degree of control over the environment.

JP: Yes. Some people in the Green movement say that the anthropocentric view of life is correct and that all we need to do is to manage our resources more efficiently. Essentially, what they are saying is that utilitarian principles are not fundamentally incorrect, but that they have just not been operating as efficiently as they might be. In that context, when one is talking about a more conservationist-oriented approach to life, what we are really talking about is managing that resource more efficiently so that it meets the needs of many people for a longer period of time.

For example, from a utilitarian approach, once whale populations are restored to something like their former size, we can sustain a certain amount of whale hunting every year. There are some people who would say that it's legitimate to continue to hunt the whales sustainably from here to the end of time—taking so many per year so as not to damage the breeding population. There are other people who would say that the whole ethic is false; that the very notion of a sustainable use which requires the destruction of the whales, or any other species, is flawed philosophically and is not worth considering. I hold to the latter position very strongly. One of the problems is that much of the writing, and often the thought, that goes into the environmental movement today is still completely trapped by utilitarian principles.

CT: Is it more than just a philosophical viewpoint? Is such questioning actually affecting people's action?

JP: I think it's beginning to have an effect. Take the animal rights movement. Fifteen to twenty years ago the animal rights movement was seen as little more than a gathering of elderly animal lovers. Today animal rights is an important part of radical thought. We are asking, "What kind of relationship do we want with animals?" There is a much stronger philosophical awareness of what it is that justifies or invalidates the cause. We are challenged philosophically.

In the past, a lot of issues would have been dealt with at the level of superficial, political responses with people saying, "This policy will sort this out." That approach is no longer adequate. It's now necessary to look at things from a deeper perspective and say, "Not only have we got to do this, here are the reasons why." We have to look at our *relationship* to life on Earth. Unless we get that relationship right philosophically, it is unlikely we'll get the policies enforced that would match up with that relationship.

CT: Contemporary social-political patterns appeal very, very strongly to self-interest. The message has to go out to people to take responsibility for poverty, violence, cancer, and unhappiness in the West and elsewhere. I sometimes get concerned when we speak of a *future* crisis. In my observation, the crisis has already arrived. Genuine self-interest and global interest is the same.

JP: Yes, it's here now. It's not as if we should be sheepish in arguing about a new enlightened form of self-interest. The need to be out there, putting that to people, is crucial. On every page of the Brundtland Report [a 1987 report dealing with economic development and global change], you find justification for why we should help the Third World in order to build up *our* exports, develop relationships we haven't had before. "Do this and you'll benefit in the long run. And if you don't, watch out, because things are going to be bad."

No doubt people would say the Brundtland Report was imbued with an ethic of enlightened self-interest. I would say it's a very limited form of self-interest, and "enlightened" only in as much as it's based on the assumption that the Third World benefits economically only if we build up our markets in the developed world. The report still fails to go beyond the constraints of a materialistic interpretation of self-interest. If we talk more in terms of personal rather than economic growth, we can give people a clearer interpretation of what "self-interest" might really mean.

CT: The phrase "personal growth" is very current. Is it going to mean much to someone who lives in a high-rise apartment?

JP: It genuinely depends. There is so much alienation and unhappiness that to talk of personal growth, without, perhaps, using that phrase, certainly shouldn't be seen as elitist or irrelevant. There are ways of trying to enrich people's lives without necessarily exploiting the finite wealth of the planet.

CT: Yes. The degree of alienation is so great—people alienated from each other, from animals, from the Earth. We have a long history of being removed—physically, psychologically, emotionally, and spiritually. What is going to breach this separation?

JP: That's the crunch.

CT: That *is* the crunch, isn't it? There is the fact of alienation. How is that fact going to reach people's hearts?

JP: It depends on how you look at this. The Americans are wonderfully optimistic about it all. They use this wonderful phrase, "the quantum leap," which refers to millions of people suddenly reaching a new plane of awareness. The French are quite the opposite. They say there is this gap and we'll never bridge it, so let's just talk about what it would have been like if we had bridged it! Very depressing. I think that in the U.K. there is a rather more sanguine realism about this situation and the problems of bridging that gap.

Something that is indirectly enhancing our ability to get our message across is that all other messages are being revealed as increasingly empty and incapable of meeting people's needs, even their material needs. Some of the political promises that underpinned our life have ceased to have a lot of meaning. More positively, however, people have begun to look to other options. For example, not everybody today considers unemployment to be a scourge. Many people today look at unemployment as an opportunity to develop potentialities that could simply not have been expressed before. So people are taking the negative and seeing the positive side.

CT: People easily get burned out, experience frustration, and a loss of energy and focus. To some extent, this characterizes what is happening to society—feelings of hopelessness and helplessness. How do you guard against this?

JP: It's very difficult. People in the Green movement are just as vulnerable to either that sense of exhaustion—spiritual and physical—or indeed, to the gradual erosion of compromise, whereby people's principles are thinned out by virtue of their confrontation with reality. Those who don't base their convictions exclusively in political principles, but feel that the spiritual dimension is very important, seem to have a deeper reserve that they are able to call on. And this seems to remain intact even when they are being assailed by all kinds of depressing views and difficult questions about whether they are doing the right thing. If there is that spiritual reserve, it gives you a sense of purpose that simply lets you pass over lots of negativity in a way that you don't think you could have otherwise.

I know that I would not have been in Green politics for ten years if I hadn't felt very strongly the sense of spiritual commitment that lies behind it, not just the personal political commitment—although I don't much like to separate those things out. I've been one of those who has reasoned for integration of spiritual and political life for a very long time. I am convinced that the ideas will never establish themselves quickly enough and thoroughly enough exclusively through a political process. There is an enormous inertia built into our society which is too great to overcome without a deeper appeal to people's spiritual values. The spiritual dimension has enriched my own life, but it has also provided a backdrop for my political activities. For me, the link between politics and spirituality, as you quoted right from the start, is very close. I'm not really able, in my own mind, to separate them out. The writings of someone like Thomas Merton, for instance, have always made an infinitely greater impact on me than someone capable of skating over any political consequences of their spiritual beliefs.

CT: One might say you either have spiritual awareness or you haven't.

JP: I don't think so. I would disagree with that very profoundly on the basis of my personal experience. I have developed a feeling of reverence for the Earth and creation; I wasn't born with that. I never had it. I was brought up in a city and I used to muck around on Hampstead Heath, but I never actually felt any kind of relationship or "kinship"—to use a dangerous word!—with the Earth. And it's only gradually, bit by bit, over the years, that I've begun to develop a tremendous sense of being bonded with the Earth. I also don't think that I have had any special revelations with regards to more conventional theological or spiritual matters. I'm a blundering, completely incompetent, hopelessly unorthodox Christian when it comes to many things. I'm someone who is fascinated by Eastern mystical traditions. I am a uselessly eclectic hodge-podge when it comes to a spiritual base. What's important is an understanding of the transcendent *in life*, not a million miles removed from ordinary people. I get tetchy when people say we need to be precise about what spirituality is. As soon as you are more precise, you are laying down what *the* Green model of the spirit should be.

> "Some genuinely feel that it is elitist to talk about spiritual matters; that if you combine your political beliefs with your spiritual concerns, you are likely to set yourself above the vast mass of humanity. . . ."

CT: Once one endeavors through language to articulate the spiritual, it imposes a set of ideas on it. Yet we must recognize that spirituality includes a deep reverence for life. The Eastern traditions offer meditative ways and means for an inner spiritual renewal to take place. I've felt within the Green movement that there is not sufficient emphasis in that direction.

JP: I think you're right. There are a lot of people in the Green movement who are worried about the spiritual emphasis. Some genuinely feel that it is elitist to talk about spiritual matters; that if you combine your political beliefs with your spiritual concerns, you are likely to set yourself above the vast mass of humanity and, therefore, be less effective politically. I find this to be an extraordinary perception!

CT: The ego can very much identify with the spiritual and create an elitist and superior attitude. One who converts to any view or position is vulnerable to that kind of expression of one's ego through a certain arrogance or conceit that "I know."

JP: I can't claim to be immune from that. I am conscious that, on occasion, the way in which I will argue about the link between politics and spirituality is quite dangerously egotistical.

CT: The very awareness of that is probably the major safeguard. If you are discussing the political and the spiritual, people can hear it more easily when you say, "Yes, I have an interest in this, and my ego does get in on the act as well."

JP: I think it's important for each person to distinguish between the egotistical and the spiritual. For me, the time when I started to think deeply about the animist tradition, which has become an important part of my spirituality, began when I started planting trees in New Zealand. By and large, I got into that for good old capitalist reasons. My parents had bought up some seventy acres of land and they said the trees would be worth a lot of money in the year 2000. And I thought, "Jolly good idea." So I was out there in the wind and the rain planting trees, and I can't say that I felt anything deep stirring within me, apart from the fact that I was engaged in a useful activity that I happened to enjoy. But after three or four years, I began to develop a much deeper relationship with those trees and that land. It could have been there from the start had I been open to it, but frankly, I wasn't. Now I'm in a peculiar position of feeling spiritually very close to that piece of land and not very interested in the financial implications of it.

CT: In that respect, we've come full cycle into the transcendence of the material.

JP: That's right. I am encouraged by the extent to which people *can* change even if they are closed off from things. Most people have not chosen this, but gradually they have had options and potentials taken away from them. Most people don't actually understand the ways in which their lives are being impoverished in nonmaterial ways. When you read an author like Jeremy Seabrook, for instance, he writes a lot about changes in working class culture and impoverishment of many different kinds, including the damage done to our culture by a loss of direct participation in the arts.

CT: Now just to go back for a moment, you referred to your experience in New Zealand and, obviously, this period of time has had an impact on you. To some degree, these types of experiences influence the course of one's life, but few people have either the time or opportunity to have that kind of access.

JP: I know. It's difficult to make any sort of response to that because I'm conscious of having had, as you have, an extremely privileged opportunity to be alone in contact with nature. For the most part, I don't reflect a great deal in my daily life; I'm usually very busy and don't have much extra time, which is one of the things that most upsets me. But to be alone for three months or so, which I have done now on four or five occasions, has mattered enormously. Without those periods I honestly don't think I could sustain the things that I do now. But again, that is a privilege. Where do people find access to solitude in our society today? One is either lonely or overcrowded. The two things seem to cancel each other out.

CT: Solitude can be found by participating in meditation retreats and workshops, or getting out to the countryside. I love my visits to London, although I don't come very often. There is a dynamic energy here with so much to be discovered in the people, the buildings, the parks.

JP: Yes. We are never immune from the power of the Earth.

CT: But so often we want to separate the city from the Earth.

JP: I know someone who I would consider to be in closer contact with the Earth than I'm ever likely to be. He lives in

London and has access to one small house. And yet, I would say his relationship with the Earth is as rich and as beautiful as anything that anybody could aspire to. He makes no fuss or nonsense about it, and he's not particularly interested in theoretical abstractions about his relationship with the Earth. He simply lives it.

The Religion of Consumerism

An interview with Sulak Sivaraksa

In August 1984, during a period of martial law, Sulak Sivaraksa, Thailand's internationally respected activist for peace and social justice, was arrested by the Thai government on charges of *lese-majeste* (offending the monarch). Sulak had made statements in a taped interview such as, "I think the king should be looked upon as a human being who exercises his power judiciously but is nevertheless fallible. If I wish to attack the ninth king, I must write during the reign of the ninth king. I don't have to wait for the next."

In Thailand where reverence for king, country, and religion is traditional, Sulak's comments were used as an opportunity to silence his influential voice. He was held for twelve days in a top-security detention center. He was due to be tried in a military court and faced between three and thirty years imprisonment. There would be no appeal after sentencing, and observers would not be permitted to witness the trial.

There was an international outcry over his arrest and the trial procedures. Amnesty International, peace organizations, aid agencies, religious leaders, universities, and lawyers around the world and in Thailand protested. The Thai interior minister said at the time, "The law is Thai law. Foreigners must not interfere with our judicial process."

On November 30, Sulak and two codefendants, the interviewer and publisher, appeared in court and were informed by the presiding judge that the public prosecutors wished to withdraw the case. Afterwards, Sulak said, "It was a good period to test my spiritual strength and to learn to appreciate one's friends and well-wishers, both at home and abroad. Prayers were said for us regularly by Buddhists, Christians, Hindus, and Muslims. We must really help other victims of injustice as we all live on this tiny planet Earth."

Sulak, who is married and the father of three children, is a lawyer and social analyst. He campaigns for and lectures on nonviolence. He is coordinator of the Asian Cultural Forum on Development and chairperson for the Thai Interreligious Commission of Development, as well as a member of the international board of the Buddhist Peace Fellowship. A number of his books have been published in English, including *Siamese Resurgence, A Buddhist Vision for Renewing Society,* and *Siam Through a Looking Glass: A Critique.*

Sulak interprets the contemporary crisis in both spiritual and social terms. He speaks out against corruption, communism, nationalism, capitalism, and consumerism. He speaks for the renewal of the countryside, the value of constructive criticism, the necessity to support and protect the poor, and the application of Buddhist principles to social reality.

Not surprisingly, he has been in trouble regularly with the authorities over the years. In 1976, while speaking in England, he read in *The Times* of a warrant out for his arrest in Thailand. During a military takeover, his bookshop in the heart of Bangkok, opposite his home, was raided by the police and army, accompanied by television and press crews. Thousands of his books were burned, rendering him almost bankrupt.

I interviewed Sulak at his home in Bangkok, where he had lived for forty years. In September, 1991, Sulak was forced to flee Thailand after the military government issued a warrant for his arrest; he had again criticized the government, this time to his students at Bangkok University. At the time of this publication, it was still unsafe for him to return.

•

CT: In recent years you have seen the enormous impact of Western consumerism on Thai society. Since you have lived in both England and Thailand and have some awareness about

Western culture, please say a little about this impact.

SS: You must realize that Thailand, which I prefer to call Siam, was not colonized, which is a blessing. But we have been more harmed than those countries which became colonies of the West. At least our neighbor Burma, which was colonized, resists Western consumerism. Unfortunately, Thailand never resisted the West because we thought that we maintained our independence. First we were colonized intellectually by adopting a Western way of living, but we still preserved our political independence. At first these Western intellectual colonizations only took place among the Thai elite in Bangkok. The rest of the country was more or less free from this form of Western colonization, partly due to Buddhism and partly to our indigenous culture.

CT: When did this influence of Western intellectualism begin in Bangkok?

SS: Sir John Bowden came here in 1855. He forced the open door policy and so we signed the Bowden Treaty with England. King Mongut, internationally known through *The King and I,* was a Buddhist monk for twenty-six years. He was wise because he knew if we did not open our country we would be colonized by the British. So he opened the country to the British, and at the same time he invited the French, Swedish, and Germans, to balance the situation. So politically, although we were not equal to the West, we felt superior to our neighbors who were colonized by the French, British, Dutch, and Americans. Our first downfall was to look down upon our neighbors.

We thought we were equal to the West. In fact, we wanted to be equal to the West, so gradually we followed the West. We invited the English lady, Miss Anna Leonowens, to teach children here. King Chulalonkorn sent all his sons to be educated abroad. When they came back, they still retained their Buddhist heritage and Thai culture, but they admired the Western way of life. They gradually introduced Western education, medicine, technology, and administration. Correspondingly, this reduced our indigenous education and culture. Buddhism as the state religion became formal, like the Church of England, and lost much of its sanctity.

CT: There has been an acceleration of the values of consumerism in the last twenty years . . .

SS: . . . Thirty years. At least the old culture maintained a certain *noblesse oblige*, but the new elite, devoid of the old culture, just want to be rich and powerful in the name of development. They just want to expand in every direction, including cutting the country up through road building. In the old colonial system, the British and the French tried to maintain themselves. They thought they would be in this part of the world forever. On the one hand, they had to respect us, and on the other hand, they had to maintain the environmental balance. The West thought it could get our timber forever. They replanted the trees so there was not much destruction of the forests. But then the Americans came. They have a very short-term view. They wanted to get the natural wealth of the country out as quickly as possible. The American period coincided with the development of Bangkok and the rest of the country. With the American period came the age of advertisement—the age of the consumer culture, which claims to be a universal culture. So a decadent Western culture was brought to Thailand, along with sexism, violence, and the use of drugs by the young. If you come to Bangkok now, you can see the new kind of temple in the form of the department store. People flock there.

CT: Bangkok looks just like any Western city. One goes outside of Bangkok and one can still sense rural Thai society. Is the shadow of Bangkok penetrating into the rural traditions?

SS: Yes, unfortunately. Development is another word for greed. Our city people never owned land up-country. We never had absentee landlords before. In this age of so-called development, the developers want more land and so destroy more forest. Our education teaches people to admire the urban life, the civil service, and business. So obviously we brain-drain our rural areas. If you go to the villages today, you find old people. The young, who have mental power and ambition, are leaving the villages for Bangkok. If you cannot compete in Bangkok, you may go the Middle East to sell your labor. We even export our women as prostitutes to Germany, Japan, and Hong Kong. The minds and bodies of the young are exploited.

CT: These are all signs of the erosion of a society. Isn't there a danger of idealizing traditional rural society and values and seeing all the fault in Western consumerism and its values?

> "We offer what we can to each other. We use the word *sahnuk*, which means to enjoy our life in a relaxed way. In the traditional Thai culture, play and work are part of life; competition is not to be admired but cooperation is."

SS: There is a danger if you romanticize it. Rural society was not all that ideal, but it was self-sustaining. People respected one another; the young respected the old. In every Thai village there was a temple which was a center for spiritual, educational, and cultural activities. The self-supporting village had been functioning for at least 700 years in this way. It wasn't ideal, but it worked. The Buddhist philosophy has a central principle that it is noble to give rather than take. We may not be very good Buddhists, but we practiced generosity [*dana* in Pali, the early Buddhist language]. We offer what we can to each other. We use the word *sahnuk*, which means to enjoy our life in a relaxed way. In the traditional Thai culture, play and work are part of life; competition is not to be admired but cooperation is. This approach worked. In this view, those who lived a virtuous and ethical way of life, like the monks, were very much appreciated. At the same time, there was respect for other forms such as animals, birds, fish, and trees. Within my lifetime, there has been this major change.

CT: Why is it that self-supporting, self-sustaining societies have simply not been able to withstand the pressure of consumerism and that consumerism becomes the predominant religion? Why is consumerism so powerful that it eats into every worthwhile value?

SS: You have to realize that consumerism represents greed. We all have greed within ourselves. Consumerism is basically linked with feelings of power, elitism, and a sophisticated kind of education in science and technology. In fact, power represents aggression and anger, and we all have that. The new educational system teaches you to be clever, but not wise. In fact, we create delusion in ourselves and we think that it is knowledge. Unless we understand the root causes of greed, aggression, and self-delusion, we get bogged down. Consumer society works like magic on the mind. It deceives you into believing in the value of consuming more, going faster, living in greater convenience. It sounds wonderful, but you do not realize the cost. I feel that once people realize the negative aspects then the situation can change.

CT: Are people realizing the negative aspects?

SS: One of the good things about this country is that more and more people *are* realizing this. There are positive aspects to the consumer society, but there seem to be more negative aspects. Once we realize this, we can resist it.

CT: There are then two realizations. One is the force of greed, aggression, and delusion, and the second is the realization of the impact these forces have on society and the planet.

SS: Being a Buddhist, I have to see everything with *upaya,* that is, with skillful means. The Buddha taught that the first thing to be aware of is *dukkha,* unsatisfactoriness, or suffering. Once you understand that consumerism brings *dukkha,* you find the causes for *dukkha.*

CT: The friend who drove me here today is a businessman in Bangkok. He was cheated two years ago by a business partner of one million baht. He is still suffering today over the situation.

SS: Unless the man looks into himself and into the causes, the suffering continues. You have to translate the essential teaching from your spiritual tradition to confront the modern period. Otherwise, Buddhism is nothing more than a decoration, which most governments would like it to be. Paying respect to the national religion and holding big ceremonies may be useful, but at the same time could be more harmful. We can apply the skillful means of the Buddha to understand suffering and social reality and the way to be free from suffering. Through mindfulness, nonviolence, and Buddhist practices, there is the possibility of overcoming suffering, both personally and socially.

CT: What are the skillful means for social change?

SS: The good thing about this country is that it has been a Buddhist kingdom for a long, long time and is one of the few left. The Buddhist heritage is available in almost every village, although many villages have succumbed and only the form is left. But there are still many villages which have the form, content, and local spiritual leadership. I know this country. I live in the capital. I have also been exposed to the West. My job is to tell people of the ways available to overcome their suffering and the unsatisfactoriness in life. I work on myself and my society. I look to spiritual leaders who have mindfulness and awareness themselves. I have met quite a few who try to have a positive answer.

CT: Can you give me an example of engaged spiritual leadership?

SS: In Surin province in the northeast of Thailand [the poorest region of the country], an abbot remembered that when he was young, people were also poor, but he sensed that there was more happiness at that time. The people related to each other much better and there was that *sahnuk* feeling among the people. In the environment, there was plenty of jungle and the elephants roamed the region freely. The people were free and were able to rely on themselves and the environment. They produced food for their families and for the monks and nuns. What was left over, they sold. They had the four prerequisites of food, clothing, shelter, and medicine. In the last thirty years, through constant development, there are more highways and roads. The jungle has disappeared, the elephants have disappeared, except for the elephants kept for the tourist to photograph. The people suffer.

CT: What was the abbot's response to all this impact upon Surin?

SS: The abbot said that something is seriously wrong. Consumerism means capitalism; it means money comes first. "Our local resources go to Bangkok, the multinational corporations, and then to the superpowers," he said. "This is useless and wasteful." He felt that there must be a way to confront things together and solve things together. He said that we must use the old traditions.

CT: Are people expressing interest in that approach?

SS: Oh yes. This is a success story. When he started, people didn't believe him, but because he was a monk and meditation master, they would come. He pointed out to them what went wrong. He said, "Let's try alternative ways of living." He even used strong words like "communal farming." In this country, consumerism came along with anticommunism. If you use such concepts as communalism or communal farming here, then you can be accused of being a communist. But when a monk who is pure in conduct of body, speech, and mind speaks this way, he arouses interest among the people.

CT: Obviously the role of the monk is important in terms of the renewal of deeper human values.

SS: The old customs and values must be translated into the contemporary setting. Today people are suffering a great deal. People were told that their traditional values were no good. They were told not to use the buffalo for farming but instead to use the tractors. People were fascinated with technology. Hired labor occurred with bigger farms, instead of small self-sufficient competitiveness and, therefore, brought more and more suffering to village life. The monk said that the people have been brainwashed into this way of thinking and living.

CT: What alternatives is he suggesting?

SS: He is encouraging the people to farm together, to share their labor together, and join together. Skillful means also have to be applied to every area of rural life including the shortage of rice, the unpredictable weather, and the destruction of the jungle and forests. The abbot said we need to have a rice bank instead of going to the bank to borrow money. The Temples can start the rice bank—whatever is cultivated and left over from eating is offered to the temple. The temple keeps the grain. Anybody in need receives the grain from the temple free of charge. It is a new kind of merit-making translated straight away into social reality.

CT: How do the people respond to this?

SS: Very well. The temple has become powerful and serviceable to the people. The next project the abbot started was a buffalo bank. Being Buddhists, we don't like to kill the buffalo. The temple keeps the buffaloes and offers the offspring of the buf-falo to the people who can't afford to buy them. The condition is that the buffalo must be treated kindly. Half of any future offspring must be returned to the buffalo bank.

Up until 1973, we were told that we were the last of the free lands. We had to fight the communists and believe in

Americanism and consumerism. We had been brainwashed for so long. Young people started questioning that. In 1973, the students rejected the American model, but unfortunately they went to the other extreme, to the Maoist model. So we were in danger of jumping from the frying pan into the fire. Hence, in 1976, the military came back into power with the blessings of the Americans and Japanese and began killing our students. Other students fled to the jungle. Others joined the Communist Party of Thailand under the influence of the Communist Party of China. That bitter lesson taught the students that Communism was not the answer; it was a fake. They have come to see that the social way of life of their ancestors and what the Buddha taught is truly meaningful and can be applied in the present time.

CT: You are speaking of the Middle Way—between the two extremes of capitalism and communism.

SS: That's right. We must turn the society towards social justice. We must change both ourselves and our society. There are, of course, monks not in touch with the modern world, both in a positive and negative way. Sometimes when they are not in touch they have insight and wisdom to give us. Others who are not in touch with the world hang on to outdated ceremonies. Again, we have to use skillful means to distinguish the sheep from the goats.

CT: You have been consistently outspoken in your public lectures, meetings, and writings. How free is free speech in Thailand today?

SS: To be fair to the government, compared with all our neighbors in Southeast Asia, we are much more free. We can speak our mind on almost any subject, except perhaps the monarchy.

CT: Did you tread on the toes of the government when you voiced criticisms in 1984? What you said and wrote brought you before the military court.

SS: The pretext was that I said something against the monarchy. I feel if the monarchy is to survive it has got to survive like the Western kind of monarchy. It is not that I admire the Western monarchy, but I think it survived because it could withstand criticism. To me, criticism is an essential teaching of the Buddha. I criticize the Buddha too. The Buddha welcomed criticism of him and his teaching. He instructs that we do not accept anything unless we scrutinize it.

CT: In a healthy society, criticism must go into every area, even those areas regarded as sacred.

SS: I don't accept sacredness, you see. As a Buddhist, I revere the Buddha more than anybody else. Even so, he is not sacred. I respect him profoundly, but even his teachings should be criticized.

CT: In the time you faced charges for your criticism of the monarchy, there was strong protest from the West over the charges.

SS: To be fair, the King was also a little bit embarrassed. He was educated in Switzerland. He is a man who would welcome criticism personally.

CT: He does tremendous work for the rural people and the hill tribes.

SS: Without doubt, he has very good intentions, but with some of his good intentions I disagree. We should be able to spell out differences openly.

CT: You have spoken in this interview about what has happened to Bangkok. Why do you choose personally to live in Bangkok? Why aren't you living in a rural society?

SS: Partly, my own roots are here in the city. Former generations of my family were in Bangkok. I feel that my role is as an urban person. I can learn from the rural area for the benefit of Bangkok, and I feel that Bangkok is the place were we suck everything from other areas. We must change the people of Bangkok so that they respect the people in the rural areas. That's my job. As part of my job as coordinator of the Asian Forum on Development, I had to work in the whole region. I feel that if you want social justice in any village, you can't do it in one village. The work has to be linked to other villages; one country has to be linked with other countries; the Third World has to be linked with the First World. We have to build up that understanding and use the Buddhist methodology of *kalyana mitta,* that is, good friends, who are on a similar wavelength and have a similar understanding. We must help each other. The small fishermen must help the working women; the working women must help the industrial workers. Somehow we must all start relating to each other.

> "The West has to learn how to relate truly in an equal way to the rest of the world. The West must recognize that it has a lot to learn from the rest of the world, as much as we have to learn from the West."

CT: Are there *any* messages coming from the West which are valuable and healthy? Does the West have any part to play in the so-called Third World?

SS: The good thing about the West is that it is now realizing the harmfulness that it has done. This is a very good sign. A monk who has committed harmful acts must ask for forgiveness. Since the eighteenth century and the Age of Enlightenment, the West has believed it has had the answers. The West believed it must conquer everybody else and nature too. Now more people in the West are saying, "No, our knowledge is limited. Our thought does not go very far at all." I think that is very profound. I think awareness and understanding will help Thailand and other countries tremendously. The West is just starting to become humble. More people in the West want to learn from our rural cultures. This is wonderful. Second, the West is beginning to explore spiritual depths, not only appreciating Buddhism but also inquiring into its own Christian background. Christian mystics have very profound things to say to us, which the West has denied in the last 200 or 300 years.

CT: What else do you appreciate from the West at the present time?

SS: The West has developed a certain kind of method and organization as a kind of network which we must learn. For example, the Christians have the World Council of Churches which brings together Christian activists from around the world. We have the World Fellowship of Buddhists, but it is just a kind of club. The West is willing to confront the power blocks, like the multinational corporations. This is wonderful. We must learn to organize ourselves in this way, too.

CT: What would you say the West must truly learn about itself?

SS: The West has to learn how to relate truly in an equal way to the rest of the world. The West must recognize that it has a lot to learn from the rest of the world, as much as we have to learn from the West.

CT: You are saying that there is an opportunity for fresh forms of dialogue, not based on a colonial and patronizing attitude?

SS: This is very essential. I feel my own drawback. I don't know the Middle East and yet I would like to. I would like to learn from the Muslims. I have learned from Indonesia, which is Muslim and nearer to us. Certain sections of the Muslim community there have inherited from the Buddhist tradition. We are related together quite closely. We have to learn in this day and age from each other.

CT: As an organizer of spiritual and social activism, how do you get by financially? Who gives you the funds?

SS: When you organize at the national and international level, the money comes from the West, mostly from Christian organizations. European Catholics and Protestants have been generous. I tried unsuccessfully to get some funds from the Buddhists of Japan. Fortunately, we have been able to raise more money within Thailand itself. People usually make merit here by giving money to the temples, but too much money is spent on building temples and on useless ceremonies. People are collecting money for increasing social awareness and understanding. I hope that in a decade all the money will come from within Thailand.

CT: That will be another expression of being self-supporting.

SS: Yes, that's right . . . . I am very glad to talk with you. You are an example of bridging our part of the world with the Western part. You came to learn from us and you also come to teach us. I think that this is a very good new dimension. It must be developed further.

Life Brings to the Doorstep the Field of Action

An interview with Vimala Thakar

We are the weavers of the fabric of modern society.
We can weave love, truthfulness and peace
or we can weave hatred, mistrust and war.
We will have to wear whatever fabric we weave.

Vimala Thakar is an international speaker on spiritual, social, and global values. She has had numerous books published, including *The Eloquence of Living, Spirituality and Social Action, Meditation—A Way of Life,* and *The Mystery of Silence.* One of Vimala's characteristic features is that she has refused to follow any of the traditional paths of spirituality. Her teachings are unusually free of religious ideology and religious language.

In the winter of 1956, Vimala, who is from Maharashtra in India, visited Krishnamurti in Varanasi. She had studied philosophy, understood Sanskrit, and had a wide variety of religious experiences. She had walked through the villages of India to reclaim land for the landless under Vinoba Bhave. She became friends with Krishnamurti and listened to his teachings, not only in India but also in London and Saanen, Switzerland. Vimala became deaf in one ear in 1960, and she was said to have been healed when Krishnamurti placed his hands on her head, an uncharacteristic action for him.

People at Krishnamurti's gatherings appreciated Vimala's insights and wisdom whenever she got into informal conversations with other participants. Out of these small meetings came invitations for her to speak in other parts of the world.

In India, she actively promoted the Vinoba Bhave Land Gift Movement, and currently she supports the Jeevan Yoga Foundation for village self-sufficiency.

Vimala says that human beings need to be "vitally committed" to discovering truth and delving to the roots of social injustice. In her book *Spirituality and Social Action*, she writes:

Living is something which is done in totality.
A flower which is blossoming unfolds every petal.
The beauty and the scent which were hidden in the bud
come out completely.
A fruit when it ripens grows ripe in totality.
But we human beings grow partially, in fragments.
If we have the urge to live fully, totally,
as marvelous, complete, mature expressions of humanity,
we must meet life sensitively, alertly
with each day that dawns.

I met with Vimala in San Francisco. She was facilitating camps in the United States, where people would spend several days with her, listening to talks and spending periods in meditative reflection. She has held such camps at her home in Mount Abu, India, and in Europe, Australia, and South America.

She gives the appearance of smallness and frailty, but this belies her presence. She is an eloquent speaker, both privately and publicly, both in the words she speaks and in that which is beyond words.

When we explore life's wholeness, untouched by words,
when we live in its freshness, its limitlessness,
we see for ourselves the sacred, the holy,
without which life has no meaning.

•

CT: What is the importance of observation and what does this mean in daily life?

VT: We need to observe what is happening to our minds while we move through relationships. It is only through observation that you understand what is happening inside. Understanding requires encounter with facts, and observation leads you to the perception of facts.

CT: If in my observation I see the fact, I might say, "Well, I observe the fact of my anxiety, my fear, my possessiveness, but it doesn't seem to make a great deal of difference to the fact. Why isn't it changing or fading away?"

VT: Most probably you aren't allowing it to fade away. We justify the existence of our weaknesses in the name of psychology. We justify and defend it, and thereby we prevent it from dropping away.

CT: So one must be willing to let go.

VT: Yes. Then one would become a religious inquirer. A religious inquirer is one who is willing to discover the truth and not allow anything to come between the truth and oneself. That is being religious.

CT: We can be willing to let go and yet it can still remain extraordinarily difficult—psychological pain, emotional pain, confusion, fear. I wonder if there are any other factors which essentially contribute to this letting go upon seeing the fact.

VT: I think if there is purification on the physical level through proper diet, simple living, austerity in speech, and so on, there will be sensitivity. Without this preparation, the event of dropping away of age-old weaknesses and distortions doesn't take place. It can't happen. That's why self-education is necessary. When there is an urge for personal discovery of truth, I think the quality of religiousness gets activated. Religion is a personal discovery.

CT: You are saying one has to see for oneself, not get it second-hand. How can one safeguard oneself against not becoming dependent on you or on others who are speaking about the realities of life? That always seems to happen in religious life.

VT: It happens in religious life if one wants the easy way of accepting authority and escaping from the responsibility of personal observation and discovery. If you want the easy way, then you go and follow someone and fall in the trap. What is more important is the love of freedom, the desire to exercise one's own initiative and not to bargain and give away your freedom for anything.

CT: So your function is to put the focus back on the person.

VT: That's right. Lead a person toward his or her inner life, not make them dependent upon me.

CT: Would you say there are far too few teachers who do that? The tendency seems to be toward dependency, authority, religious leaders, gurus, and so on.

> "If you want the easy way, then you go and follow someone and fall in the trap. What is more important is the love of freedom, the desire to exercise one's own initiative . . . ."

VT: This commercialization of religion and spirituality is the curse of the day. We are living in a commercialized civilization. So religion and spirituality are also misused, abused. A new relationship between the inquirer and the person who understands is necessary.

CT: What are the dynamics of a balanced relationship?

VT: I have used the term "the nonauthoritarian way," which I use to refer to a way of communication. I communicate with you and you communicate with me in a nonauthoritarian way. A simple person who has arrived at enlightenment can be misused by those who are craving to find an authority. They become dependent and relegate the responsibility to that person. That is our pattern of life.

We have to stimulate the urge for freedom, an urge for learning. If we can stimulate these two things among the people we come across then they will know that freedom is something which cannot be bargained for. You know, freedom is not something you sell and then get something in return for, not even liberation and enlightenment. The transpsychological value of freedom should be emphasized, as well as respect and a reverence for life. These are the essential things.

CT: I would like to go back to observation and meditation. In observation, the heart and mind come to quietness rather naturally or effortlessly. And there comes within that movement a meditative state of being.

VT: I would say silence rather than meditation. Between meditation and a state of observation comes the dimension of silence, a total emptiness. So observation leads to that total emptiness. Silence is the dimension of innumerable energies. Modern man is so fatigued and exhausted, even for a man with a cultivated mind. Before he can act in the so-called outer or social field, he has to discover in his being a new energy. The dimension of silence provides one with the release of such energies.

CT: Taking the example of a monk's life, the monk leads a rather simple life with a certain purity of speech and an awareness of diet. The monk observes and is aware of his relationship to the world and there is a quietness in his life. Monks come to a certain silence and emptiness, perhaps, either through the absence of method and technique or not. Energies may get released, yet they may not be visibly manifesting in the world.

VT: What do the monks do, then?

CT: Live very quietly and simply. Some monks live in total isolation and some are in a monastic setting.

VT: That's not living. Once you remove yourself from the

mainstream of relationships and withdraw into isolation, physical or psychological, you have stopped living.

CT: Are you saying that the monastic system in which monks and nuns live is inadequate?

VT: They create an artificial world. They create a world for themselves and live there. If you withdraw for the sake of study, investigation, and exploration, one can understand that. But if you create a pattern of isolation, whether it is monastic life or any other life, you cut yourself away from the challenges of life and relationships. Western or Eastern, in every setting, the desire for security keeps people isolated mentally.

CT: So what will contribute to our being less isolated?

VT: It is the willingness to be vulnerable to life, whatever it brings; to meet life. Living is to move with the challenges of life. Meditation can give us a greater capacity to meet these challenges. So it is vitally necessary to go into retreat. We need to wash out all the toxins that get into our psyche when we are exposed to the inhumane stress and strain of modern life. Usually people go out for vacations. If instead they go out for retreats they will come back revitalized and reenergized, provided they do not fall into the trap of any sect or dogma.

CT: In a way this is a new and refreshing approach—to step out of the world for short periods. It's not like the life-long monastic system, it is short-term. One is nourished so that one can live clearly in the world.

VT: Yes. It's like inhalation and exhalation. You inhale vital breath when you go into retreat or occasional silence. You are inhaling the energies. Then when you go back to your relationships and your so-called world, you are exhaling. So it's a cycle of inhaling and exhaling.

CT: In giving consideration to the total sphere of life, you include political action.

VT: Not power politics, but people politics.

CT: Would a person need to include this dimension if one's life is to be total?

VT: Not artificially. Everything gets included according to one's inclination. Somebody may be an artist and they will function through their art. Somebody may be a musician and they will utilize their capacities. And the same with literature, dance, economics, and political work.

Through silence and meditation the center of the "me" disappears completely. You are nothing but emptiness covered by flesh and bones. Then it is life universal which uses such a person according to its capacities, strengths, talents, etc. It is not for the person to decide what course of action he or she will take. Life brings to the doorstep the field of action.

CT: So, out of the emptiness, there comes such a degree of receptivity that one doesn't actually have to look.

VT: That's right. One doesn't have to choose. It comes.

CT: For people involved in peace work, one of the difficulties is the degree of aggression and negativity of some of the people involved.

VT: Then it's not peace work. If the minds of the workers are not peaceful, then they don't know that peace is a total way of living. If the peace has not altered the quality of their motivations and the texture of their behavior, then they are not peace workers. The existing peace movements may not have a spiritual foundation. Every action should have a spiritual foundation, or egoless consciousness, or the dimension of awareness. They will have to find out ways and means of working for peace. Then they will be working out of compassion and not out of any ambition.

CT: Would you say that, in a total sense, work on oneself is a prerequisite to outer work?

VT: Absolutely so.

CT: Some may say that it is a prerequisite to be a totally prepared human being. But the world is in such a crisis and in
such danger, should I keep preparing myself, or should I bring
the inner and outer work together?

VT: I think the person is under some illusion. While I am
preparing myself for mutation, or transformation, I am contributing to the world of peace. The very act of self-education
is an act of tremendous service to humanity. When one human
being transcends the bondage of the ego, or "I" consciousness,
they become a living cell of something new which is going to
spread from their center. So it is not that while you are preparing yourself you are not contributing. There is no dichotomy
between the two.

CT: I agree. But the structure of society says that unless you
are seen to be visibly doing something, then you are not contributing. This is a Western idea.

VT: That's the problem of society; that's not our problem.

CT: What would you say are the factors in daily life which
contribute to transformation? For example, how important do
you consider contact with like-minded people?

VT: If the religious inquiry becomes the common point which
brings people together, then I think it will be very wholesome.
How do you create that contact with like-minded people in
daily living? How do they come together? What will be the
basis? Is there a person or an ideology around which they will
rally? Or will these like-minded persons or inquirers come
together only because they are inquirers?

There is the necessity for such people coming together;
we have to function in this manmade world. So if we get one
another's support, moral and psychological, it becomes easier
for us. But how do the people come together? Up to now they
have been coming together around a person. They are more

with one person than with one another. So individuals are rallying around a person, around an ideology in the framework of an organization or sect. But free individuals as inquirers or religious persons coming together in freedom, on the basis of friendship and common inquiry, is something which is not seen in the world.

CT: To some degree people rally to you, not necessarily as an authority figure, or as a cult or sect, but they still rally to you. Without someone who has deeper understanding, can people really rally with each other?

VT: That's my hope. For tomorrow.

CT: Would you say that meditation is an absolute essential for clear action, even though fears arise when we see the tendencies of mind and when we go into the unknown?

VT: Meditation is a way of living.

CT: Therefore, it is neither inner or outer.

VT: That's right. It is total. It's a totality that moves within, in relationship to a totality that is outside of you.

CT: Often the mind creates the idea of seeing the totality in a passive way, not an appreciation of the active quality of being *in* the totality. How do we come to an understanding that is not just seeing totality as a meditation state?

VT: Totality is often regarded as a rigid destination. But it is a beginning of new life where there is no division of the "me" and the "not-me." There is a quality of a new perception and quite a different quality of responses. So the movement of totality means the movement of egolessness.

People have created an entity out of totality, out of God, out of liberation. As if there is something out there to reach. But it is not a fixed point, not at all.

Dealing with the Death Squads

An interview with Joe Gorin

Joe Gorin is fond of calling himself "Buwish." In the last twenty years, a number of Jews have traveled extensively, particularly to India and the Far East, to explore other religious traditions. This is not a case of dismissing their religion of birth, but rather exploring the depths of the spiritual life. Such people have come to be referred to in a light-hearted way as "Buwish"—a combination of Buddhist and Jewish.

Joe Gorin was born in Cambridge, Massachusetts, took a degree in psychology and became a psychotherapist, working in a clinic and in private practice. He took part in his first intensive insight meditation retreat in 1978.

During his years of spiritual practice, he came to realize that unresolved emotional and psychological forces influence political actions. He perceived that there were people in this world with immense political influence who were basically living out their unresolved problems around violence and fear.

Joe became a member of the national board of the Buddhist Peace Fellowship and participated in meetings to discuss nonviolence both as an ethical foundation for spiritual life and as a strategy. He also participated in a number of campaigns to halt Washington's support of right-wing regimes in Central America.

I remember participating in a small group meeting of peace activists in a private house in Leverett, Massachusetts with Joe, two prominent political activists and organizers, Paula Green and Jim Perkins, Dave Dellinger, who was one of the "Chicago Seven" put on trial twenty years ago, and other activists involved in the Witness for Peace campaign. We saw a film of a Contra attack on a truck in Nicaragua. Some of the activists, including Joe, had traveled to the borders of Nicaragua and Honduras to witness for peace. The witnesses would stand in the hills of the trouble spots and live in the villages, and thus inhibit the Contras from launching attacks on the people who lived in the region. It was well-known that if U.S. citizens were harmed in a war funded by their government and right-wing businesses, the American public would demand an end to support for the Contras. It was a high-risk strategy, but it saved lives, and the witnesses could report back to the international media what they saw.

In 1987, Joe decided to quit his job as a psychotherapist and work in Guatemala to give personal support to those threatened by the death squads. He also spent time in Nicaragua and El Salvador.

Joe has written a book on his experiences, *Choose Love: A Jewish-Buddhist Human Rights Worker in Central America*. He has also spoken at numerous meetings about the situation in Central America. "The nine-year-old girl I saw in the remote village of Cuatro Equinas in Nicaragua was killed by bullets that were paid for with our tax dollars."

In August 1989, he returned to the United States, and immediately after his return participated in a retreat with me at the Insight Meditation Society in Barre. It was at this time that I recorded the interview.

Joe now lives in Holyoke, Massachusetts, where he works as a psychologist. He works primarily with people from Central America, particularly Puerto Rico. He also counsels people who have tested positive for the HIV virus, and children who have been sexually abused. He is the former director of the Network in Solidarity with the People of Guatemala (NSGUA).

•

CT: Nine days ago you returned from Central America. What was your intention in going to Central America?

JG: I went there in July 1987. I had been working as a psychologist for ten or eleven years, doing a great deal of psychotherapy, training students, and consulting with community agencies. I started coming to the Insight Meditation Society in 1978, about the same time I started doing psychotherapy. During all this time I was politically active, since the Vietnam War. Insight meditation informed my activism to a great degree.

In 1984 Erik Kolvig, Paula Green, and I formed the Western Massachusetts Chapter of the Buddhist Peace Fellowship. I later joined the board of directors of that organization. We organized a trip to Nicaragua with the Fellowship of Reconciliation. I became increasingly active in Central American issues in the early 1980s; a close friend of mine had been abducted, tortured, and killed by a death squad in Guatemala in 1980. That altered my interest a great deal. He had been there for four years at the time of his abduction and assassination.

I started to relearn Spanish. I had been around it a lot as a kid, so it came back to me fairly easily. I became involved in issues around Nicaragua and El Salvador. A Salvadorean refugee who had to flee that country lived at my house because I was the only person in the neighborhood who spoke Spanish. I also became involved with the local Quakers, who were giving sanctuary to a couple of Guatemalan refugees. My passion was the struggle in Central America. It became clear to me that my full aliveness was not happening in my work as a psychologist but in issues of Central America.

So I had lived there for the past two years, when I led this delegation of Buddhist Peace Fellowship and the Fellowship of Reconciliation people to Honduras and Nicaragua. Then I started working for Peace Brigades International, an international group based on Gandhi's concept of nonviolence, born out of the conflict between India and Pakistan. Civilians would interpose their bodies between conflicting armies. Today Peace Brigades in Guatemala works with people threatened by death squads and paramilitary death squads and with other potential victims of political violence.

CT: These people in the Peace Brigades: were they Guatemalans or from overseas?

JG: There were no Guatemalans. It was considered unsafe for Guatemalans to join this particular group. Guatemala is concerned about its overseas image, particularly in Europe and North America. The death squads involved in disappearances and assassinations are somewhat loathe to involve North Americans and Europeans for fear of tarnishing their image in those places.

CT: What kind of numbers have disappeared in Guatemala?

JG: In 1954 there was a popularly elected government which the CIA led a coup against. In the last twenty years there have been 100,000 political extrajudicial assassinations and 40,000 disappearances. There are about one million exiles and internally displaced people—this means that the people were forced to move to some other part of the country or escape into the mountains to flee the army.

CT: Does Peace Brigades have an office in the capital or is it a secret organization?

JG: The headquarters is in the capital city. They also have established a center in Quiche Province. When I started with Peace Brigades we only had one person who would go up to the Quiche, probably the most dangerous area. I was that particular person. I spent a moderate amount of time outside the capital, working specifically with a couple of people. One man, Amilcar Mendez, is frequently threatened because he is leading a group trying to dissolve the Civil Patrols, which are these legalized paramilitary groups. The government has created these compulsory Civil Patrols of civilian males, between the ages of fifteen and fifty. It is a key part of the counterinsurgency. The Guatemalan constitution states that these are voluntary. In fact, they have about 800,000 men involved and virtually all of them have been threatened or intimidated into joining.

So, I did a lot of work with Amilcar by accompanying him when he had to go on dangerous missions.

CT: Did Peace Brigades International give you any advice, training, or instruction?

JG: Yes, we had a training period. We had a lot of reading to do beforehand and we had weekly team meetings to discuss the situation. There were people from the Grupo de Apoyo Mutuo [relatives of the disappeared—literally: "Group for Mutual Support"]. We would frequently accompany members of that group, one of whom was six years old. She is the daughter of the president of this group. This little girl received frequent death threats. We had to accompany her almost twenty-four hours a day. Her father had been disappeared by security forces when she was an infant. She was targeted because of her mother's political activity. We also had much contact with workers. At one particular plant occupation, we had a twenty-four hour presence.

CT: You speak of accompanying somebody around the clock. What does that mean?

JG: Sometimes we would accompany them from their house to their place of work. For example, we would accompany a teacher to their school, stand outside the school for three, four, five hours, then accompany them back home. Somebody might want to meet a coworker downtown. We would look around to see who was in the restaurant. Did anyone look fishy? We would want to know where the exits are.

CT: Did you put out that you were North American and not a Central American?

JG: There is quite a noticeable racial difference. The Guatemalans are considerably darker, so there would be little likelihood of that confusion. But, it was known that a lot of the people we accompanied were highly visible. They were in the newspapers all the time. The death squads, the government, and the military all knew these people were being accompanied by internationals, either European or North American.

CT: How do they feel having you like a shadow with them all the time?

JG: Usually there was a very warm and loving relationship. But there was one particular person I used to accompany who resented her escorts. I started having thoughts like, "This ingrate doesn't deserve me," so I could see quite readily that all my motivations were not coming out of humanitarian and political dedication. Part of me was doing this because I wanted to be loved and appreciated. That gave me cause for considerable self-reflection. Of course, I came to understand why someone might feel aversion to being constantly shadowed by someone.

CT: Were there situations where there was a real threat?

JG: During the first eight or nine months in Guatemala I worked with Peace Brigades, then in the Nicaraguan war zone and then for another period in Guatemala. During this first period, I was the chauffeur for a group of four exiles who came back, one of whom was Rigoberta Menchu. [Rigoberta Menchu was nominated in 1992 for the Nobel Peace Prize. At the present time she is a leading figure in the "500 Years of Indigenous and Popular Resistance" campaign. There is a movie about her called *When the Mountains Tremble.*] These four very highly visible political exiles were front page news in Guatemala for weeks before they came home. Their whole arrival was one of the most controversial things that happened in Guatemala. There were lots of threats against them. Security was very tight. Rigoberta was arrested on arrival but immediately released due to international pressure. I was chauffeuring them around and they also had a police escort, so I had to make sure that the police were following me. It is not very reassuring to know that some of the police who are the authors of these tragedies are your protectors. On another occasion a student activist was murdered. Her sister, who looked almost exactly

like her, was frightened she might be a target. She was trying
to get out of the country fast. I was accompanying her during
her last days in Guatemala with the probability of death squads
looking for her. At one safe house we heard what sounded like
someone trying to break in. On numerous occasions I was approached in the street by strangers asking me who I was or what
I was doing. It was hard to tell whether I was being paranoid
or not.

CT: What is the channel for threatened people to get out of
the country?

JG: The common way is what they call *mojado* [wet]—just
going illegally through Mexico and into the U.S.. Canada has
a program to take in people who are threatened by political
violence. One must be able to prove it. The murdered woman,
whose name was Elizabeth, had gone to the Canadian embassy
about a year before saying, "The death squads are following
me. Can you get me out of the country?" She could not prove
it, so they did not get her out. Amnesty International also in-
tervenes. I was working with a woman recently whom Americas
Watch helped to get a temporary tourist visa to the U.S.. Sixteen members of her family have disappeared or have been
murdered. The death squads were combing everywhere for her
to make her number seventeen. However, her U.S. visa is only
good for a year.

CT: How did you take care of your food, money, health, and
accommodation?

JG: I had room, board, and fifty dollars a month from Peace
Brigades. I also received donations from international friends
who believed in what I was doing and wanted to support me.
    On one occasion I had gone to El Salvador. Peace Brigades
has a team there; I had gone to translate at an international
meeting. My first day there I went by the U.S. Embassy. It is
a fortress. There is a fence with electrified barbed wire on top,
and a sheer mass of concrete wall. On the wall there is all this

wonderful high-quality graffiti. One said in Spanish, "Aqui se planifican los masacres del pueblo Salvadoreno" [This is where the massacres of the Salvadorean people are planned]. It says this in big letters on the wall of the U.S. Embassy. I knew that it was a No-No, taking pictures of embassies and military, but I could not resist. The coast looked clear, I pulled out my camera, took a photograph, put the camera back in my backpack, and was feeling very smug when all of a sudden I found myself surrounded by Salvadorean police. If my mission here was found out by the Salvadorean police, it could compromise the security of Peace Brigades. I acted like a dumb tourist, which came distressingly easily! "Oh gee, I'm sorry." They took my passport. I travel with nonpolitical books, I had Jack Kerouac's *On the Road*. I'm alternately reading this and wondering about life in a Salvadorean prison. They had gone over to the embassy. Two guys appeared, clearly C.I.A.—sunglasses, casually dressed—and suggested I enter the embassy with them to be interviewed by the U.S. Consul General. I have a number of friends who had gone with the Salvadorean police, so I said, "Sure, I'll talk to the Consul General." I continued to behave like a dumb tourist. "How long do you plan to be in El Salvador?" "Two weeks." What was my work? I said, "Psychologist." I began to bore him to tears with details about my career. He invited me to a wine and cheese party they were having right there. I said, "No thanks!"

CT: What were your feelings towards him?

JG: I spoke to the Consul General for about half an hour, during which time I came to like him. He became more of a human being than a Consul General. This brought up for me a dilemma that I had to wrestle with many times during my two years in Central America: how do I reconcile the fact that this is a fellow human being, with frailties, fears, and loves, who I find likeable and engaging, with the fact that he is a mildly important cog in one of the world's most oppressive security operations?

People in El Salvador are very much at risk. There are a lot of arrests and detentions. We received a communication from a group of Guatemalan exiles who had found out about aerial bombardments of the civilian population in the northern part of Quiche. So I was selected to go up to the northern part of Quiche in the Ixil Triangle. It is a conflict zone. I went up to the military base and knocked on the door and said, "Hi, is the Commandant home?" I met him and we spoke about aerial bombardments. According to our reports, and to eye witnesses whom I spoke with, the army was bombing civilian populations. The civilian population of the area had fled to the mountains to escape the arbitrary massacres. The army wanted these people back down from the mountains because they wanted to have them under their control. These people were reputed to be the social base of the guerrillas. Guatemala has the longest standing continuous guerrilla insurgency—about twenty-eight years—in the hemisphere, if not the world. The army would go up with helicopters and, using people's full names, would say, "Come back to Nebaj [the principal town]. If you don't come back we are going to bomb this area." The Commandant was this charming, funny, intelligent guy who, like the Consul General, I couldn't help but like, although I knew this man was murdering civilians. My goal wasn't to get him to stop bombing. It was to advise him that the international community was aware of what was happening. They have to then take this into account.

CT: What was the response from the Commandant?

JG: The moment I sat down in his office, he went right for the jugular. He said, "What is the legal status of your group in our country?" We don't have legal status. So, I deftly handled that one: our application actually got up to the President of the Republic's office. The President did not want to be the one to reject it, so he sent it back down and asked them to reject it, but it hadn't been rejected yet. I said, "The only thing we are waiting for is the President's signature." One develops a different sense of right speech in such situations!

CT: Did you ask him directly about the bombing?

JG: I asked about the bombing. He said, "It's not true. Don't believe it. Don't believe everything you read." Then he said, "Do you know who Rigoberta Menchu is?" I said, "The name sounds familiar." He said, "Menchu! She says we are trying to commit genocide. Sixty percent of the population is indigenous, so if we were to commit genocide, we would have to kill just about everyone. Genocide is completely impractical!" Being Jewish, I get very nervous when I hear talk about genocide being impractical. There is a quiet genocide going on in Guatemala, 100,000 murdered, the vast majority of whom are indigenous.

> "Being Jewish, I get nervous when I hear talk about genocide being impractical. There is a quiet genocide going on in Guatemala, 100,000 murdered, the vast majority of whom are indigenous."

There were times when I wanted to kill him, and I suppose he wanted to kill me. Yet at other times, he was very human. The fact that he was not a personification of a Hollywood villain made it harder to deal with.

CT: During your time in Central America, you sent out a considerable number of letters.

JG: I was sending out about one letter a month. These were pretty thick letters—they were about eight single-space typewritten pages about my perceptions, my experiences. They were cathartic for me and also let people know what was happening. It was also a form of my giving back something to the literally hundreds of people who had supported me during this time.

CT: So, from Guatemala you went into Nicaragua. Once again to meet with the Peace Brigades?

JG: In Nicaragua I was working with Witness for Peace, which is a different group. It is a Christian group. I am a Jewish Buddhist. People were interested to see what a Jewish Buddhist looked like. I began to develop a great appreciation for the model of Christian-based communities. The communities gather together to reflect on the teachings of the Bible and act on those reflections.

CT: Is it born out of the insights of the liberation theology movement?

JG: Yes. One of my sources of optimism for Central America and Latin America is the reawakening of the church which is happening through liberation theology. I actually was able to make sense out of the Bible for the first time. I developed a great appreciation for the life and teachings of Jesus. My mother would get very nervous if she knew this! Hard-line Marxists say owning class and working class are in inherent conflict; they can never work it out. Christian democrats say there is no inherent conflict; they just have to communicate better. Liberation theologians give a different perspective. They say it is in the interest of the wealthy to stop oppressing and using people. People can't be free until the oppressed person is free.

CT: Liberation is not separate from interconnectedness.

JG: The freedom of us all is in fact interconnected. No one of us is free until all of us are free. Dharma teachings influenced me in a very real way. Working with Central Americans I came to see my liberation is tied up with the freedom of Central Americans and with all oppressed people. I wasn't working so that Guatemalans could be free, but so that we could all be free, all be liberated. I was often exploring interconnectedness and how my fate and their fate were one. I have never been in the mainstream of society, but I have never felt oppressed.

There I had to work very discreetly. I got the sense of what it is to be oppressed. I saw the way the wheel turns: now I am part of a privileged elite, now the wheel turns and I am part of an oppressed group. I came to identify the part of me that has always been oppressed and that has always had some natural resonance with those who are oppressed by systems.

CT: How do actions reveal interconnectedness?

JG: For example, by boycotting Coca-Cola we feel a connection with people in South Africa—it could end up someday being the privileged elite. I think this is what Jesus meant when he said that a rich person can't enter the Kingdom of Heaven any easier than a camel can pass through the eye of a needle. I think what he was saying was that as long as one person is benefiting from the suffering of others then the Kingdom of Heaven is not available. We all profit from it if we live in the U.S., Europe, South Africa, or Australia.

CT: In Nicaragua, these communities exist alongside a continuing threat from the Contra. What was your relationship to both?

JG: I lived in the war zone, known as Region Five. It is the part looking toward Costa Rica, not far from Bluefields. The Contra are quite active there. I would see a U.S. paper and I would hear the war was over. Unfortunately, the Contra hadn't read those same newspapers! There was a lot of Contra activity—kidnappings, attacks on villages, thefts on the roads. I had three basic functions: documenting human rights abuses, taking delegations around the war zone to meet people, and "standing with the people." You once pointed out that we are human beings, not human doings. We were being with the people, living the lives they were living. We had a very good network of information about how the war was affecting the civilian population. About 40–45,000 people would receive our information in the U.S.

CT: How do you document human rights abuses? How fearful are the people of actually communicating what is happening?

JG: I didn't see that much fear from the people in Nicaragua. I saw a great deal in Guatemala. One has to earn the confidence of people who are loath to speak. In Nicaragua, people take automatically to Gringos because most North Americans in Nicaragua were supporting the people in the war zone and working against the policy of the U.S. government. People in the area thought that everyone in the U.S. were dedicated, peace-loving people and that Ronald Reagan had nothing to do with the people of the U.S.. They wanted people in the U.S. to know what happened in their little tiny villages. When there was an attack, we would talk to witnesses, to survivors.

I remember once, in the town of Jacinto Baca, we had to take an hour-and-a-half bus ride and then walk four hours. Between where the bus stops and Jacinto Baca the Contra had done about five kidnappings in the week preceding and had mined the road. We had been sent to find out the details because there had been several witnesses. In the war zone there is always rifle fire. Usually a soldier fires into the bushes to make sure it's not somebody who is going to shoot him. My coworker said to me, "Gee, I hope we don't get kidnapped. Tomorrow is my birthday." Later I was writing my monthly letter and I realized that was a fairly peculiar thing to say. At the time it did not seem peculiar at all. What would we say to the Contra if we were kidnapped? It was a relevant question because Witness for Peace people had been kidnapped three times by the Contra.

CT: Do you ever question how effective your work is?

JG: In the U.S., we tend to judge effectiveness in terms of short-term results. For example, many activists became burned out when it took years of work to bring the Vietnam War to an end. Many bought into the myth perpetuated by the media and the power elite that the end of that war had nothing to do with internal dissent. Subsequent revelations indicate that both Republicans and Democrats feared that if the war were not ended, there could be massive social upheaval in the streets of the United States that could threaten their hold on power. But if we look for short-term results that are defined by external changes, we are doomed to feel ineffective. If I need Ronald Reagan to change in order for me to feel effective, I have created a structure designed to guarantee ineffectiveness.

But when we take the long view, we can see that the tide of history is rolling toward liberation. Since the nineteenth century, we have ended slavery, achieved women's suffrage, and instituted child labor laws. The women's movement has made giant strides in asserting the full dignity of women, racial discrimination in the States is illegal, and the U.S. can no longer overtly support puppet military dictators or involve itself in prolonged troop invasions. To feel ineffective, we have to deny history. Of course, many activists break out in hives when they hear these things. They would respond that sexism, racism, militarism, and exploitation are still rampant. While this response is accurate, it denies the historical process of which we are part.

> "When there is danger, one can respond with the simple recognition of danger. That is different from fear. I would recognize danger and take whatever precaution was necessary."

CT: How do you deal with fear?

JG: I and other coworkers truly realized that fear is just a conditioned response. When I was surrounded by constant potential danger, I began to develop a different response. I remember having heard people say that fear is our friend because it lets us know when we are in danger. I don't buy that; I don't buy it in my own experience. When there is danger, one can respond with the simple recognition of danger. That is different from fear. I would recognize danger and take whatever precaution was necessary.

For example, just a few days before I left, I was involved in a potentially dangerous situation while trying to help get my friend Fladio Panteleon out of the country. He worked with the Coca-Cola Union in their theater group. This theater group for campesinos [peasants] lampooned the army. One night, after a performance, he was surrounded by men who shot him in the foot. After that he and his brother had to leave their home. His brother, Rolando, a friend of mine, was later abducted, tortured, and assassinated. Death squads were looking all over for Fladio. Canada and Amnesty International interceded. He was going to get out. We then found out that the death squads were asking nearby for him. We had to get the family out of the area. At this point Fladio, his wife, and two little boys, aged three and one, moved in with me. It very often happens that somebody just about to leave gets assassinated.

We found another house. I borrowed a vehicle from a delegation I was working with and I asked four of them to volunteer for this mission. The mission was to get his family into the van, hidden, and driven to the safe house. We knew the street was being watched. Everyone from the delegation volunteered, but there was only so much space in the vehicle. We put on our sunglasses and cameras so as to look and behave like tourists. We picked the family up, whisked them into the van, drove past the new safe house several times to make sure it was not being watched. Fladio and the family are now in Canada, along with two other people from the theater group. What was most interesting about this was that everyone in the van was fully aware of the danger of what we were doing, and yet no one was afraid.

CT: Did your years of experience in insight meditation and as a psychotherapist play a part in your own relationship to your activities in Central America?

JG: The insights which have come to me through meditation are the very foundation of the way I am in the world. The difference between what is often called "spiritual practice" and the actuality of who I am and what I do has become increasingly merged. My activities in Central America were every bit as much a part of my spiritual practice as sitting meditation. The Buddha and other great teachers have pointed to the importance of the development of compassion. It seems to me that compassion without action is pity, and pity is a characteristic that rigidifies the boundary between self and other. This is not what the Buddha was talking about.

CT: How would you describe your spiritual practice in Central America?

JG: In a conscious way, my work of these past two years has been a loving-kindness meditation. But my actual "spiritual" path took particular forms over this period. I found it very difficult to do formal sitting meditation in a war zone, although I'm sure it could be done. It is hard to just note "hearing, hearing" when what I was hearing was an AK-47 submachine gun being fired a few hundred yards away. But when I would meet people like the U.S. Consul General in El Salvador or the commandants of El Quiche, my first general reaction was to try to wish them out of existence, because I felt that their "jobs" involved the institutionalization of the three mental poisons of greed, aggression, and delusion and that they were responsible for widespread suffering. But I would not accept this reaction on my part as being any more or less solid than "hearing, hearing." I would try to see the Buddha within them, although I often failed. I would often reflect on how one can participate in a liberation movement without creating an us-and-them. I accepted this question as a sort of Zen koan.

I want to encourage people to act: look at what the next step is. It might be to write a letter to a Congressman, to work with others, demonstrate on the streets, resist taxes, go to jail, or go to visit these areas of conflict. I always viewed my work in Central America as a support for people serving others here.

The word *protest:* the etymology is *pro,* meaning for or in favor of, and *test,* meaning testify. Protest means to witness in favor of. Another word is *conspiracy: Con* means with, and *spire* means to breathe. The etymological meaning of that is to breathe together. I would just like to close by saying, let us continue to conspire to protest.

The Staying Power of Spirit

An interview with Ram Dass

In the early 1960s, Richard Alpert was regarded by his peers as a bright Jewish intellectual all set to reach the top of the academic ladder. That was until he swallowed his first psychedelic tablet. In social terms, it cost him dearly. He was a professor of psychology at Harvard and he was asked to leave. He left in 1963 and was barred from the American Psychological Association. For the next four years he was a proponent of psychedelics.

He soon realized that though psychedelics got the user high, he or she didn't stay there. "It was clear you had to do something else to become what you could taste was possible," he told me. In 1967 he traveled to Iran, Pakistan, Nepal, and India. "I finally ended up at the feet of my guru, Neemkaroli Baba." (Neemkaroli is the name of a railway station in India. The name of the guru refers to the spiritual brother, *baba,* who lives near the railway station!) He was given the name Ram Dass, which means Servant of God. After practicing hatha yoga, raja yoga, and studying the *Bhagavad Gita,* he wrote *Be Here Now,* which sold a million copies and gave Ram Dass worldwide recognition. He has since made a number of return visits to India.

In 1973, he initiated the Hanuman Foundation, which has given birth to many worthwhile projects, such as the Prison Ashram Project, which includes a massive correspondence program connecting people who are in prison with people in the outside world. The Foundation has also sponsored projects and workshops for the dying and their families and friends. Over the years, thousands of people facing death have received love, support, and honest counseling through these workshops. In more recent years, Ram Dass formed the Seva Foundation, which serves as a vehicle for compassionate action around the world. Primarily, the foundation has taken on the gigantic task of ending blindness in Nepal. Through fundraising in the United States, American doctors have been flown to Nepal to save the eyesight of countless Nepalese. The foundation also encourages self-employment of Native Americans by promoting their arts and crafts; Native Americans experience one of the highest rates of unemployment in the Western world.

Ram Dass's books have reached a wide audience in the West. They include *The Only Dance There Is, Journey of Awakening, Miracle of Love, How Can I Help?* with Paul Gorman, *Grist for the Mill* with Stephen Levine, and *Compassion in Action* with Mirabai Bush.

Throughout the years he has spoken to massive audiences in the United States. I once went to listen to him in a college hall in Cape Cod. More than a thousand people filled the auditorium. He sat crossed-legged on a backless chair and for three hours touched upon every conceivable aspect of spiritual life, including devotion, service, knowledge, action, and religious experiences. He loves relating his personal stories from the East and West and never appears to tire of telling the same stories about himself he has told on countless occasions. He is thought-provoking, exceptionally eclectic—being very supportive of the variety of spiritual practices and therapies—and very funny. He is known for his immense and sustained devotion to his guru and for his work in the service of God.

I met with Ram Dass at the Insight Meditation Society in Barre, Massachusetts, where he was spending six weeks in meditation. To his credit, Ram Dass has not rested upon his laurels. He continues to participate in workshops and retreats given by other teachers both in the East and in the West. He presently lives in San Anselmo, California. Despite being one of the most charismatic and public figures in spirituality, he continues to make himself and his personal life accessible, warts and all.

We agreed upon a forty-five-minute meeting. In fact, it ran for three hours. This was the first of my interviews, recorded when Cold War feelings were at their most intense.

•

CT: What happened when you came back from India in 1968?

RD: I continued teaching, which at that time was an amalgam of my training as a psychologist and my involvement with meditation, Hinduism, and drugs. I had to keep on listening to how they all fit in. I didn't want to go back to the role I played with the drug scene in the sixties.

One day while I was spending time at my father's farm, I went to town in my father's big car and some young hippies came up to me on the street and said, "Are you the connection that came up from Boston with the acid?" I said, "No, I'm not that kind of connection for you." I invited them to visit the farm and they brought their friends. Then they invited their parents and their parents brought their ministers. Soon there were 300 people dropping in on a weekend just to sit around and talk dharma under the tree. Some of them wanted to stay around, so my dad said they could stay up on the hill. We had a community of about ninety people living in treehouses and tents, with a meditation hall that we built.

After that I started to lecture around the country. My first lectures would last up to eight or nine hours. In 1971 I went back to India to be with Maharajji [Neemkaroli Baba]. He said to me, "No ashrams, no monasteries," which has saved me from being in the hotel business many times! In the seventies, spirituality became very big. It became attractive to the upper middle class, primarily Jewish and Protestant. They were very comfortable with their affluence but somewhat dispassionate about it. After some time, people began to realize that, though they could taste the spiritual possibilities, it was going to take effort and patience to realign their lives. The West is not noted for its patience.

The fad started to pass in the late 1970s and the numbers started to go down for the most part. The Buddhist tradition began attracting the very intelligent and committed, but for many others the fad came and went because their level of devotion was too superficial.

CT: What about the overall interest today?

RD: After the Vietnam involvement there was a lot of despair about political action. A lot of people were looking for things to do outside the mainstream of society, so they came to spiritual things. Now once again there is a kind of idealistic involvement in social-political action. It is a spin-off from the fear about nuclear energy and nuclear weapons. There is also a cynical materialism, which has given rise to the yuppies, which are the young upwardly mobile people. It is materialism with a vengeance. Economic insecurity affects whether people turn inward or not.

Older people are showing much more interest in spiritual awakening after having finished most of their working life. This seems to stem from having gone through many life experiences already. They are more mature. I'm quite interested in working with forty, fifty, sixty-year-old people. This is partly because of my age. I am fifty-three. I am interested in the elders of society and how we can honor them, and how they can honor themselves. For the most part, we have knowledgeable people in our society but not wise people. The elderly are often rejected and put out to pasture. Since I'm still outside the establishment, I have been working with rejected groups for a number of years. They are not going to give me their children to work with, so I work with prisoners and the dying and now with older people.

CT: In a way you are in a rather unusual position. You have one foot well-grounded with the establishment and the other with the non-establishment.

RD: You are exactly right. Being an ex-druggie makes me accessible to a whole section of society. I've been to the East, which makes me accessible to another section. I've got a Ph.D. in psychology and I was a Harvard professor—that makes me accessible to another section. I am bisexual, and there is a whole segment who love me because I am one of them.

CT: What is your view on the teachers who are coming from the East?

RD: Christopher, you've been in the East, as I have. We know what a "real" teacher is. From my point of view, "real" teachers can do anything they want to do because they are "real" teachers. What we have now in the West is not necessarily the cream of the crop. The teachers who came to the West often wanted something on the personal level. There was a tendency in the 1970s to elevate anybody who came along and say they were a guru and then project onto them. We were building them up to cut them down. This is what we often do with our politicians. It is almost like a ritual sacrifice. We give them a year or so of power and then burn them.

So many teachers see themselves as bearers of the truth, the truth that will set people free, and everything else is some sort of bastardization of that. The ego gets involved. The teacher has a vested interest in transmitting something. They are not interested in the peace and harmony of the world. They see that as a very short-term thing. They see the world as a place of suffering and they want to give birth to a method that will last. They want their students to be preoccupied with the lineage, so they don't lose it the minute he dies. It's a hard job, a damn hard job.

If a teacher is transmitting a lineage and you go in with a pure heart, you can receive the teachings rather than the lineage. You can get the teachings and they get *their* own impurities. You don't have to worry about their impurities. They have to do their own work. All this can do is force people to trust their hearts more. You go for the teachings rather than the teacher, and you see teachers as teachings, rather than as teachers.

CT: If the emphasis is on maintaining the tradition and the methodology, mixing with global realities would certainly be watering it down, but if it is encouraging the spirit to come out . . . .

RD: I understand. Then the question is: Where is the practice in relation to the spirit? Is the teacher responsible for the transmission of a lineage of practice, or for the touching and emerging of the spirit?

That is interesting. I'm in the spirit business! I'm not a Hindu. I'm only interested in spirit.

CT: The way you were speaking before, you sounded more sympathetic to the transmission of lineage than the transmission of the spirit.

RD: What I am saying is that the staying power of spirit is in part dependent on the input from rigorous practices.

CT: Do you see yourself as a transmitter of the lineage stemming from your guru? This lineage may have handed teachings from guru to disciple for generations. Are you the successor?

RD: The predicament is that it is very hard to enunciate that lineage. It has no form. He would say, "Meditate!" and then he would disturb you and laugh at you when you meditated. It is the form of love and service, I guess. It's a peculiar system to transmit. He said to me, "Go, do it!" but he didn't give me any tools except to love everyone, serve everyone, and remember God. I realized by the middle seventies that in some way I was going to have to embrace worldly life in order to be free and embrace my humanity, whatever that meant.

CT: You then began to get more involved politically?

RD: I saw that every time I got involved in political action, things rose up in me that made me feel so useless—in the sense of being able to do something to bring the end of suffering— that I would retreat back. I wasn't ready. But now I see that was my work. Christ speaks of "being in the world but not of the world." I saw that I now had to be *in* the world in the sense of honoring the various identities, such as being a member of a family, a nation, an ecosystem, a species, a religion, etc.

CT: You were getting encouragement to get involved?

RD: Allen Ginsberg kept encouraging me. I had been thinking at the time, "When Maharajji wants me to do this, it will feel intuitively right." And it was beginning to. For example, about three years ago, I was in Boulder to give a lecture and I got a call from Allen in New York. There was going to be a demonstration at Rocky Flats, which is a big nuclear center near Boulder. The Buddhists were going to have a meditation out there. He was supposed to be the front person for it but he couldn't

> "My tack is that the only way that peace work works is if the work is done by peaceful people. To be a social activist demands that you work on yourself harder than ever."

go. Could I go in his place? So I found myself sitting on a zafu [a meditation cushion] meditating in the middle of this scene, feeling like I was in the right place at the right moment.

Another example. A couple of years ago I decided to enjoy my humanity. I was in San Francisco, sort of hiding out. I didn't want to be Ram Dass. A minister of a church asked me to be his guest on a Sunday morning and speak from the pulpit. I had never spoken from a pulpit before, so I agreed. He mentioned a date, which I forgot about. Now, I'm in San Francisco cavorting about and I get this message that he is expecting me on Sunday morning. I was up all Saturday night and now I'm hung over. I want to be asleep, but I go to this church. It turns out it was Peace Day at the church. The Buddhist monks who were walking around the United States for peace were there. I just wanted to go home to bed. I was wiped out, but I went ahead and I did my rap. As I was leaving the church, somebody said, "The monks are going to lead a march across the Golden Gate Bridge today. Are you going to be there?" I thought, "Oh my God, I'm wiped out. I've been up all night." So I said, "No, I have something I have to do." Then somebody said, "Somebody as important as you must be busy." So I get in my car and start to drive home across the bridge. It is a beautiful sunny day. Then I think, "Gee, it would be kind of nice to join them." Those were the ways that I started to get involved. I joined the march just as another marcher and as soon as I got there they asked me to speak. It felt wonderful.

CT: You speak about peace in your public talks?

RD: Yes. My tack is that the only way that peace work works is if the work is done by peaceful people. To be a social activist demands that you work on yourself harder than ever.

CT: There was previously a polarization—you either work on yourself or you work for the planet. But you can work for both.

RD: A lot of people who were political activists in the sixties and anti-spiritual have done a lot of work on themselves since then. All of us realized we were lopsided. So there is a coming together.

CT: Chogyam Trungpa [the late Tibetan meditation teacher] once said at a conference, "There will be no nuclear war." I feel such statements give a false feeling of security.

RD: That's interesting. I share Trungpa's feeling that there is not going to be a nuclear holocaust. I mean, a major holocaust. There may be some Three Mile Island errors.

CT: Being European, I have a different feeling. Green activists used to say, "The resources are going to run out." Now we say, "Time is running out."

RD: Fear as a motivator is not a satisfactory way to get rid of the cause of nuclear weapons. I take to task all those who use fear as a motivator for social action. "We're all in it together," is the horizontal organization instead of the vertical. For me, Casper Weinberger [then secretary of Defense] is me. The world situation is me. As long as we are separate, all motivations for survival as separate entities are going to color our perceptions. We are not going to be able to deal with the root of the nuclear weapon issue.

CT: I'm not sure there is the awareness of the subtlety of your perception. Rather than seeing the Casper Weinbergers as threats, workshops are taking place where the concept of enemy is seen to be a mind creation.

RD: There is no enemy. It has to do with where you stand in relation to the universe. If you stand anywhere, you are a perpetuator of suffering. I'm not interested in symptoms; I'm interested in the root cause.

I live in a slightly different worldview than you do. I'm not in the numbers business. Gandhi says, "Make yourself into zero and your power is invincible." I'm interested in that domain as much as how many numbers there are in a peace movement. The fabric of world thought is very fragile. A thought can change it just like that. And one event can change all of the thought of the whole system. Shifts in thought have to occur. One of them is by a few people being without fear. There is a purity that can be fed into the system. What Gandhi and Martin Luther King brought into the system was the quality of their being, not just the ability to organize people.

CT: You and others have expressed faith in the unlikelihood of nuclear war. For us in Europe, we have the feeling that we just don't know. The security in America over the years has produced a certain optimism.

RD: I have a very close friend. His name is Emmanual and he is not embodied. He is an extraordinary being. I told Emmanual that I work with dying people and asked him what should I tell people about dying. He said, "Tell them it is absolutely safe, like taking off a tight shoe." When someone asked about the nuclear threat, he said, "Don't be silly. School won't be out that soon. How presumptuous to think that they could destroy the world."

CT: This is an American disembodied spirit!

RD: What Trungpa, Emmanual, and I intuitively sense is that the shared awareness of the horror of our predicament has permeated enough into the world that there is less and less likelihood of that happening. Although, it might happen by error or by terrorism.

CT: I think that Trungpa's analogy of two guys, Russia and America, with a knife against each other's throat is a very powerful image. Everybody surely realizes the implications of the situation by now.

RD: I believe that behind the bluff of the poker game there are people who are very much pragmatic, survival-oriented, and functional in their way of looking at the universe.

CT: Are you referring to the people in power?

RD: Yes. I realize that I just lost the peace movement with that statement. However, I think these people in power are rational beings who are caught in power roles in which they must sound and act a certain way, but that act does not involve the destruction of the world. I'm certainly not in favor of these people being in power.

In some ways the bomb has already fallen. We are all living with death over our left shoulder; it's never going to go away. We will never undo the knowledge of how to build the bomb even if we get rid of all the bombs. We are just now figuring out what it means to live with death.

CT: Have you been to Europe recently?

RD: No. I do understand that the feelings about the Pershing missiles and all of that are very different there. I live in a rela-

202 • *Spirit of Change*

tively protected, isolated country. I don't know whether my feelings about a nuclear war are coming from that conditioning or another place in my being. From my own personal point of view, I do not think it is going to happen. We must listen to the fears of the people who are building the arsenals and help them to devise strategies for feeling safe and independent of nuclear weapons.

CT: As I listened to one of your public talks, I felt you have the capacity to please people, which makes the listener very attentive to what you have to say. When you mention your views to a broad spectrum of people, it may reduce their fears and anxieties about a future nuclear war and so reduce their personal suffering. But, simultaneously, it makes a person feel a bit more comfortable and in that, awareness can fade.

RD: I just said my views into a microphone knowing that those were not popular views. Obviously, I'm willing to say it. That's the first thing. The second is that I told you that I do not work with fear as a motivator for social action. You are asking me not to say something because my saying it will dissipate fear. I agree with you—it will dissipate the fear, because I think social action can come out of another place in people. When I was standing with a million people in a demonstration in New York, I didn't experience people in fear, but a lot of people saying, "Enough, enough!"

CT: Isn't it just a speculation when you express confidence about the future?

RD: I hear the point. What I notice is that the first reactions people have are fear and urgency, and that impels an action. But, it doesn't have staying power. That's one of the things the peace movement has difficulty with. People won't stay in it because they are coming in out of those motives and they burn out very fast.

What I am trying to do is to resonate with people from that deeper place within. It is like we are representatives of a higher law in the universe that doesn't allow the thing to go so far off balance that it destroys itself. This is a correcting mechanism that comes from a very deep, intuitive place in people. Your point about knowing the future as a detrimental thing is well taken. Obviously I don't know the future. I live very much in the "don't know" myself, so how am I going to treat this sense I have that it is not going to happen?

CT: There was a strong belief in England before World War II that it was not going to happen.

RD: Yes. I think you're right. I think that I could make that distinction. I'm trying to support particular actions to prevent what could occur, and yet at the same time, realizing that it might occur. I'm trying to go with that motivation for action. Awareness says, "I'm part of this whole thing and I must do my part." I guess when I made those statements, they were in reaction to the fears of people. It was to undercut that. That's why I really think that I have been motivated to do that. I think it is not skillful means. I hear what you're saying and I think it is right. Of course, I don't know, but intuitively I don't think it is going to happen. That is my truth. Am I not to share that with you? That's what you are asking me to do. That's what you are saying is skillful means. I say, "It is never skillful for me not to share my truth." Do you hear the issue? I have been asked so many times to do something which is deceptive. People have said, "Look, don't discuss your homosexuality. We don't really want to hear about that." I say, "I'm sorry. That is my truth."

CT: The Buddha made reference to speech. He said, "Speak that which is both true *and* useful."

RD: There was a time at the temple when I would become very angry because Maharajji said to me, "Tell the truth and love people," but the truth was I didn't love them. Usually what I did was make believe I loved people because that was the acceptable thing to do, since I was a devotional yogi. But I decided to tell the truth for a change. And the truth was I didn't love them. So I told everybody I didn't like them and to keep away from me. I was getting more and more furious. One day I threw a plate of food in somebody's face. Maharajji was watching this and he called me over and said, "Is something troubling you?" I said, "I hate all of these people. I can't stand myself. My hatred is for everybody. I only love you." He started to cry and began hitting me on the head. He got milk and poured it on me and said, "I told you to love everybody." I said, "But you told me to tell the truth and the truth is I *don't* love everybody." He came up closer and said, "Love everybody *and* tell the truth."

At that moment I saw who I was going to be when I stopped being who I thought I was. I have been dying ever since then into being somebody who loves everybody and tells the truth. You called me on another one, you see. You said, "The truth *and* what's useful." OK. I hear it, and I hear how I have to work with that.

Recently I wrote down a "To do" list:

1. Intend to keep my heart open. Remember what Kabir says, "Do what you do with another human being but never put them out of your heart."

2. Quiet the mind so it is not at the reactive mercy of each passing thought.

3. Listen with a non-judging, non-craving awareness and to how adversarial positions are reflections of the struggles within myself.

4. Align my actions with my deepest truth, which is one of harmony.

5. Help to reframe the context and models in which situations are perceived.

6. Acknowledge my fear, anger, and frustration at the horror and uncertainty of things.

7. Reconsecrate myself again and again so that my actions will be as an offering to God by whatever name. To stop complaining and enjoy.

8. Be responsible but not take organizations too seriously.

9. Keep my sense of humor.

10. Accept responsibility for my shared stewardship of the planet, and act. As the Sufis say, "Trust in Allah, but don't forget to tie your camel to a tree."

The issue of acting out of fear and urgency without working on oneself is an interesting one. People don't realize that their greed for "this" is causing "that." If their personal life is all screwed up and they're busy fighting with people, divorcing and all of this kind of stuff, that's as much a contributing factor. We need to listen to the caring language of the heart.

CT: In the peace workshops, I ask, "What's the difference between dying from cancer from radiation fallout and dying from cancer from smoking?"

RD: Exactly. Many people's lives are often a shambles. They are creating waves of anger and unhappiness and they are justifying it all because they're busy with the nuclear issue or some other issue. To me that is very shortsighted and also, it's just not working. Someone like that is a symptom relief person, an allopathic physician, and I'm for going to the root cause.

CT: Women seem to be bringing in a strong intuitive element in looking at the root cause of suffering.

RD: When I was at Harvard in the 1960s, rational thinking was the highly valued strategy in life. Intuition was seen as a weak quality and women were seen as intuitive and, therefore, weak. This was a real put down. I was a part of that because I was part of a junta that demanded more statistics and more experimental methodology. So when I opened through drugs, it was a 180 degree turn for me. It turned out that the intuitive aspect was very harmonious with a part of my being, which is related to my Jewish tradition and my psychosexual development.

Women are bringing in new myths as well. When we look at politics in mythic structure, there is certainly the need for new myths. As we're moving from the material and analytical levels of reality, if we skip the mythic level and go too fast into the formless level, we miss a very powerful vehicle for social transformation.

CT: Wasn't the myth around a particular figure, the hero, who is going to take the flock to the Promised Land? Well, part of the message of the women's movement is that there will be no individual leaders within the peace movement.

> "Every ingredient needed to generate the force necessary to change the political reality of the Earth is already present and exists in every individual's heart."

RD: I think that the women's movement has contributed to that, but it is not the dominant determinant of it. It's a networking consciousness which works at a horizontal rather than a vertical level.

CT: Would you say the lack of the hero is a healthy facet?

RD: It is incredibly healthy. I really think people should be empowered as individuals. Representative government is second rate compared to government by the people. We are beginning to recognize Gandhi's statement: "Though what you do may seem insignificant, it is very important that you do it." That's networking. I love it.

CT: Do you see fresh ways in which the peace movement can be explored? What else do you think people can touch their hearts on?

RD: Every ingredient needed to generate the force necessary

to change the political reality of the Earth is already present and exists in every individual's heart. What is required to bring that forth is what we talked about earlier, the creation of myths. This allows an individual to acknowledge that part of themselves that previously had been lost in the shuffle—buried underneath economic, psychological, political, and social realities.

Bringing in a myth is extremely important. Let's look at Poland. Lech Walesa and some of the people who head Solidarity hold a different myth about what Poland could be, what the power of the individual is, and what the government holds. The commitment to their myth was strong enough that the government had to bow down because the myth inflamed the people's hearts; it so touched their hearts.

In the film Gandhi, do you remember the nonviolent strikers at the salt mine getting beaten up by the army? They were ready to suffer for what they believed, without reacting violently. You've got to be ready. That's Christ's message. You've got to be ready for your myth to be strong enough. So, there's the question of who is ready? That is why we have to work on ourselves. That's the essence of Gandhi's message, of Christ's message. In the last analysis we do what we can as part of groups, institutions, and movements, but the onus for each of us is to go back in, to work on ourselves, to become that instrument.

As long as there is a flickering place that wants something of the world, including life, you are vulnerable. As long as you are vulnerable, you have a price to pay.

CT: I have been reading the story of Steve Biko, the South African black activist who was interrogated, tortured, and killed by the South African police. Again, the complete commitment, the unwavering commitment.

RD: Most of the people in the social action movement are very idealistic; they're in Wonderland, and then you see how they live in their daily life and it's crap. Their marriages, their relations to other people, the drinking—it's not clean. How can they expect to be a soldier of God or be an instrument of that kind of change? That's a big demand on us. The question is whether people are ready to have that asked of them. Nothing less will work. The numbers game is a game of the world. It's not coming out of a feeling of inner strength because people have lost connection with a part of themselves that is strong, that is free. As long as you are not free, how can you free anybody? As Gandhi points out, "When you defeat somebody, you don't win."

I say, when you go out and get yourself arrested, that's making a statement that is coming out of a very deep place in you. That's a statement to make as an individual; that's wonderful. When you're preoccupied with how many people have sex with you, that is coming out of a different place. In order to make a shift, you've got to get out of the conspiracy or scenario that everybody shares. When I go to India for four months and don't read a newspaper or listen to the news, I'm doing it out of a sense of responsibility, as far as I can see, in order to really hear what's going on within.

Sometimes we look in the wrong place for what is important. I find when I'm teaching there just needs to be one student who hears and I have contributed to a balancing of the whole force in the universe and that will resonate out and out and out. I have found sometimes, too, that when I'm clear enough, I can walk on a stage, just arrange the water pitcher, put my notes down, get the chair ready, and by the time I've sat down the whole work is over. It was like mime. It was all a nonverbal communication, just the quality of being, joy, playfulness, and lightness and at the same moment, responsibility and patience.

After I sit down I say, "Well, that's the lecture, ladies and gentlemen." That's what we have to demand of ourselves as teachers, Christopher, the integrity of our beings. It's so easy to lose your compassion in the importance of what you think you're doing. There is a strategy of life where you can leave yourself open to that all the time, and there is a strategy where you can close to it because it is undermining your ego.

Life Is a Pearl

An interview with Fleana Bergonzi

One in five people in the Western world will at some time be diagnosed with cancer. Given the hectic pace in the West, it is not surprising that some of the contributing factors to cancer appear to be pollution, diet, and stress. Both allopathic medicine and alternative therapies are working to combat this disease.

I met Mauro Bergonzi, Fleana's son and a student of oriental philosophies and religions at Rome University, through his participation in a number of Buddhist retreats. He was translating various texts on Eastern spirituality from English to Italian. One of the books he translated was *The Experience of Insight* by Joseph Goldstein, an insight meditation teacher.

Fleana, a homemaker, observed that the process of meditation and self-observation was making noticeable changes in Mauro's consciousness. She had earlier had surgeries which removed both breasts. She felt certain that the cancer would not return, but in 1982 it did. It was at this time that she asked Mauro to teach her meditation. Both Mauro and his mother practiced insight meditation with Corrado Pensa, a professor at Rome University. To expand her self-understanding even more, Fleana started to meet regularly with a psychotherapist.

In some parts of the West there is still a widespread view, largely misinformed, that anyone who visits a psychotherapist regularly must be either neurotic, depressed, trapped in a phobia, or suicidal. Certainly, a therapist works with such clients, but for many who are well-adjusted to daily life, the regular meeting with the therapist is an opportunity to deal with personal pain and to find out more about oneself. The therapist has a valuable role to play in this regard.

By 1983, Fleana knew she was experiencing a life-threatening illness and that it was only a matter of time before the cancer consumed her body. The cancer began to move quickly and was carried to the brain.

Mauro and a friend, Francesca Rusciani, who acted as interpreter, took me to the Bergonzi home, a spacious apartment in Montesacro, one of the countless suburbs of Rome. The five of us, including Fleana's husband Egiolio, sat down to a lunch of pasta and wine. We began speaking together in generalities about Rome, the Pope, the weather, and mutual friends. From there we began to explore the impact the cancer had, not only on the family, but also on the neighbors, with whom the Bergonzis seemed to have a rather easygoing relationship.

Fleana was as talkative as the rest of us. The only visible sign of her illness was that she had lost most of her hair due to the radiation treatments. She was relaxed, attentive, and more than willing to share her experiences. She exemplified what in some circles would be called an "open system." At the dinner table her husband said very little except to expand or clarify a point from time to time. I could tell from his eyes that he was immensely proud of the dignity and clarity his wife had in dealing with this pervasive cancer.

Later in the day, Fleana and I sat down together in the living room and I recorded the interview with her. A number of times there were tears in her eyes as she recalled an event. There was a precious quietness as the meeting flowed on. One of the many thoughts I had during the interview was whether the clarity and expansive understanding which Fleana had then would be able to carry her through the more advanced stages of the cancer.

Twelve months after the interview, Fleana died. Mauro telephoned me from Rome. I asked him how she had coped with the last weeks and days. He told me that she was even more radiant and serene than on the day I spent with her. She had died with "an innocent smile."

•

CT: Could you tell me about the history of the cancer?

FB: It started when I was thirty-eight years old, when I had the left breast removed. At that time I felt a sense of rebellion and victimization. Eight years later I had an operation on the right breast. My reaction was very bad: I felt a lot of fear, endless fear. Three years ago, when I was fifty-six, the cancer came back through metastasis of the bones. [In metastasis, clumps of cancerous cells break off from the original mass and are carried by lymphatic vessels or the bloodstream to distant parts of the body.] The same thing had happened to my mother. So many people around me were dying of cancer. Because of all this I started to understand that something new should happen in my life, so I went to seek help because I felt that on my own I couldn't succeed. I couldn't go on living with so much fear and pain. Great help has come from my son, Mauro, who has been trained in Eastern philosophy and religion. He taught me to meditate. And there have been other wonderful people who have been really helpful to me through their love and affection.

CT: Three years ago did you expect the cancer to return?

FB: After two operations on the breast I thought that the cancer had gone forever. So for ten years I felt sure in myself that I needn't worry about it anymore. The doctors then told me that a metastasis of the cancer had taken place. There was nothing else to be done. The cancer had spread everywhere. Here and there. All the back bones, ribs, and brain.

CT: How much physical pain was there?

FB: At the beginning the pain was very, very strong. I could hardly move. I can remember some days when the pain was really intense. Doctors are often not very clear. They do not say very much about what's going on. So at the beginning my husband, son, and I spoke a lot between us about accepting the situation and coping with it. But the doctor that I'm seeing now is very clear. We had a good talk together. He told me that a metastasis of the cancer had taken place and that I had to take certain medicines, hormones. So I started to take them and the pain decreased.

CT: At that time what were you experiencing inside yourself?

FB: Something new was starting to take place in my life. I had been in a meditation group for some time with my son and some friends that I was close to. I can say that through this community, through certain books I read, through the care and love of my friends, I really jumped to another dimension. By then, I had already gone to see a psychotherapist who was also interested in working with cancer through a method influenced by Simonton's therapy.

> "I started to see myself from an external point of observation, as if I were detached from myself and was able to see how many useless pains and passions there are in life, and I started to feel more detached from all that."

CT: What was the original reason for going to the psychotherapist?

FB: I needed help to go through life and face death.

CT: What kind of meditation were you doing?

FB: Vipassana [insight] meditation, which works with the breath and body scanning. While doing the body scanning I used to stop in the areas which were most painful. I used to wait for the pain to melt down, or to move, or sometimes to become a knot. In the end, the pain used to dissolve. Then it would come back. Generally speaking, I had great benefit from the meditation. I started out looking for a physical benefit and I found a great spiritual richness. I realized the most important thing was to make every day a full day, a full and alive day. Psychologically speaking, the benefit I got was very great. What I learned is that the body and mind go very much together.

CT: So this became a spiritual concern affecting your relationship to life?

FB: Definitely. I just want to live every day as an end in itself, a treasure. I would think this before I began meditation, but then as I went on meditating I began to understand this in a much deeper way. I started to see myself from an external point of observation, as if I were detached from myself and was able to see how many useless pains and passions there are in life, and I started to feel more detached from all that.

CT: Was this feeling of being detached from everything a feeling of alienation or seeing more clearly?

FB: It was definitely positive detachment, to see my projections, my dreams, and fantasies.

CT: In the therapy were you concentrating on any area of your life, such as the relationship to yourself or to someone else?

FB: At the beginning, the psychotherapist and I began to look with care at what had happened in the periods of time just before the first two operations. The psychotherapist asked why I allowed cancer to grow in myself. I told him I felt like a martyr and a saint. I suffered a lot when my husband lost his job. I felt hurt by a great sense of humiliation. All my life I have been helping others with a somewhat blind sense of self-mortification, without really taking care of myself. So whenever I happened to suffer in life, I did not feel any responsibility for what was going on; I thought it was an external accident which had nothing to do with me, so I had to bear it patiently, surrounded by a halo of sanctity. I thought I was extremely righteous; absolute honesty and morality were my favorite virtues. Everything had to be perfect in me, especially as a wife and mother.

CT: And what did the cancer tell you?

FB: That it was all wrong.

CT: It sounds like the combination of therapy and meditation was quite essential for you in that period.

FB: It gave me the possibility to see life and other people through different eyes. First, we began working with the relationship to the cancer and the operations. Then together we inquired very deeply into my childhood, especially my relationship with my parents and the problems that I had as an illegitimate child. Then we inquired further into more recent problems, for example, being like a puppet with a mask on my face all the time. Through therapy I could gradually see certain images of myself and of my life collapse, leaving a free space.

CT: Let me get the picture right. In your childhood you were cut off from yourself, hence the mask image. The way that this manifested as an adult was by cutting yourself off from yourself by being lost in other people.

FB: Yes, definitely.

CT: So you went into meditation and therapy. What did you do next?

FB: I tried to find new interests in life. For example, I had no plants or flowers in my house, and now my home [her eyes fill with tears] is full of plants and flowers.

CT: The cancer is still present and you are replacing it with new life around you.

FB: Yes, that is true. It is like there is a workshop inside of me where I have the most pain. And from that place—especially when the pain melts down—a lot of compassion comes. Compassion for me, for others, for anybody who is suffering. It is a workshop where pain and fear turn into love for every single being who is suffering. And I feel surrounded by lots of love.

CT: Did you practice and apply the Simonton method of meditation, using visualization?

FB: Yes. I can remember an image of my mother when she was very young and beautiful. That image gave me great happiness and also physical strength.

CT: Why did the image give you that? You said that your mother died from cancer.

FB: Up to that moment, the image which had remained in my mind was of my mother being sick and weak, needing help which I was unable to give her. So a fresh image of my mother —young, beautiful, and full of strength gave me strength in myself as well.

CT: Very important. As you came fully into the present, you brought more life into your home, as expressed through the plants. That transformation also transformed your memory.

FB: Yes. The image of that unhappy, weak, sick child that I was has dissolved without giving me any more problems.

CT: As you see more life in the present, you see more life in the past.

FB: Yes, it's like that. And I found again all the beautiful things in the past that I hadn't been able to appreciate. In one of my visualizations I saw very clearly the little child I was, so much suffering—unhappy, ailing and unhealthy, not only physically but also emotionally. She was dying. In order to be sure that she was really dying, that she was finally going away from my mind I looked closely through her open mouth and saw her atrophic heart and liver. Deeply relieved, I said, "She's dead. At long last!"

CT: Seeing that this suffering child of the past was now gone, how did that affect your relationship to life, your cancer, and the present?

FB: I have grown up into love and appreciation for a human being's face, for a little animal, for whatever.

CT: You told me earlier how you had given your life to others and neglected yourself considerably. Yet you still had love and compassion for others. What is the difference between now and the time when you thought of yourself as a martyr or saint?

FB: There is a very great difference. Before there was a sense of duty. Now there is joy.

> "Another time, I realized our life is a pearl. But this could take place only after passing through a kind of agony full of crying and sobbing, which was painful and sweet at the same time. By sobbing, I was preparing the ground, the shell for the pearl to be born."

CT: The cancer is still present; it hasn't actually stopped. What is the doctor telling you now about your physical condition?

FB: I haven't asked the doctor. I feel that for each person the experience of cancer can be quite different. So there is not much point to asking doctors for a forecast. The doctors can say what medicine you can take and what treatment you can go on, but they can't tell you what the future is going to be.

CT: I would like to explore further these important experiences which you have had. You might call them "spiritual" experiences. Did these occur mostly when there was a lot of pain, or did they occur in meditation?

FB: Primarily, in meditation, especially during retreats. Things that I had been wondering about and asking myself all my life finally came to a clarification, to an understanding—the relationship with the earth, the flowers, the plants, with life itself which is flowing from moment to moment, feeling enchanted by seeing a laurel tree and its leaves, feeling deeply touched by the wonder of it. I felt the difference between mere living and feeling alive, feeling life flowing within myself, being one with the earth, with the rose, with plants and flowers.

One time, during a walk, I happened to fall down and as soon as my face touched the earth there was a moment of great communion. I felt I was the earth itself and I was its smell; I was the flowers around me; I was the bird which was filling my whole inner space with its twittering; I was the tree, and everything else.

Another time, I realized our life is a pearl. But this could take place only after passing through a kind of agony full of crying and sobbing, which was painful and sweet at the same time. By sobbing, I was preparing the ground, the shell for the pearl to be born. At that time I thought I was going to die. I was preparing a kind of shell inside myself, without knowing why. When I saw a pearl being born in it, the sobbing settled down, the pearl melted, it became a single tear, and I realized that it was my whole life. I saw my son's eyes and Corrado's eyes melting together into one light. An immeasurable sweetness surrounded me and I felt one with God.

CT: Why, at that time, did you think that you were going to die?

FB: I was tired and I thought it was time to die.

CT: After seeing a pearl dissolve into a tear and then dissolve into God, was there any relationship of that experience to the cancer?

FB: I felt that the cancer was a light which had brought me to that point. I owed it my understanding. I was feeling very thankful to the cancer. [Tears in her eyes.] Illness has given me this possibility. I feel thankful for all the good opportunities which life has given me: the meditation, the therapy, the people that I have met, the readings.

The love comes freely and surrounds me at the most difficult and most painful moments. For example, when my mind was dull and confused because of the brain cancer and radiation treatment, I would wake up early in the morning, at about five A.M., and waves of tenderness caught me and tears flew out of my eyes without knowing why. Sweet, very sweet tears. Then I used to think of all the people that were dying, or wanted to die but couldn't. I would think of all the people who felt they were not loved. Then I tried with all my heart to send them love, so that they could feel this love that surrounds all of us, this love which is freely available and comes to us as a benediction if only we let ourselves go.

CT: You are saying that the resistance and conflict with the cancer is emotionally and psychologically dropping away so that love can manifest?

FB: In the times that I was seriously ill, and keeping my attention on the breath, I used to hear a call in my bed that said, "Go beyond, go beyond. This voice gave me a great sense of freedom of getting beyond every limited space.

CT: Presumably there are still fears.

FB: I couldn't describe them; there may be moments of uneasiness, restlessness. Corrado once asked me, "Fleana, are you afraid?" I straight away answered no, but then I spent the whole following day and night inquiring into that. I haven't been able to describe a real fear. Maybe there is still some fear somewhere. I'll see it when it comes.

CT: How much radiation treatment have you had?

FB: So far I've had twenty-five applications. The radiation has been applied to the brain, which is the reason I have often felt dull and confused. Sometimes I have double vision. I think it is possible to have some kind of awareness even if your mind is confused. I felt very close to the Hiroshima victims when I lost all my hair because of the radiation. I felt close to the deep suffering of all those people.

CT: Have the doctors expressed an opinion about the amount of pain you experience?

FB: Actually, the doctor assessed that I should have severe pains in my bones. But I don't feel such pains. He was very surprised and couldn't understand it. I couldn't understand it at first, either. But now, it seems natural to me that I don't feel such pain. For two years, I have been putting a lot of energy into awareness of pain. First, I send feelings of love and compassion to Fleana. Then to the pain, and from the pain to everybody else and out to the whole universe.

The support I have has really been essential. One day in my visualization meditation my son was revealed to me as my greatest medicine. My husband, although he is an old man, has done things I have never seen him do before: shopping, cooking, taking care of the bedroom, taking care of me. The whole of his life is totally devoted to me.

My neighbors have been doing incredible things for me, too. I've been very sick for the past four months. My neighbors have been like a very well-organized community in their visits. Although they never talk about organizing the visits, everything seems to just come naturally. They are always leaving dishes of food and offering us any kind of support. One lady—I don't know her very well—is a prostitute. One day she sent me a wonderful hydrangeas plant and a big bunch of yellow roses. Then she came over with a kind of childlike shyness and we embraced each other.

CT: Your life, love, and warmth seems to be attracting life, love and warmth.

FB: I believe this.

CT: In what ways has Mauro been a support to you?

FB: Well, for example, I was sitting on the toilet and I was so weak I couldn't stand up. Mauro helped me to stand up to go to my bedroom. When I had to have the radiation he would take me there every time. I have learnt meditation from him and he has introduced me to his friends.

CT: I'm feeling very touched and nourished by this whole experience with you. We cannot feel your pain when it arises but we can feel, within ourselves, your love. Let me ask, finally, how do you regard the future?

FB: The future is tomorrow. I hope that it will be a nice day. I hope that we will be able to go out and have a walk. I shall see what I shall find tomorrow. It will be a surprise. I might find a blossoming tree, or meet somebody. I'll just see what comes. Every day brings me something new.

CT: There is the reality of cancer, and the reality of the transcendent which embraces the cancer and allows you to see so much more. Everything you have said this afternoon is a wonderful testimony to what is possible in the face of suffering.

FB: The richness that I am feeling comes from beyond and is nourishing me. And this richness belongs to everybody.

Healings in New York

An interview with Norman Rosenberg

Norman Rosenberg, coauthor of *The Healing Sea,* works as a psychotherapist, Reichian therapist, and meditation teacher in the heart of New York. It is a city where tension, anxiety, and ambition dominate millions of people's lives.

He told me once, "Living in New York is a constant challenge. On the best day, when you fly in you see this brown haze hanging over Manhattan. I get sick for two days after I have been away from the city. My body has literally to switch over from breathing poison.

"We are living in this incredibly compressed space in Manhattan with the noise pollution and people pressure. My wife [Leeny Sack], a teacher of kinetic awareness, my former wife, Laura Rosenberg, and I decided to open a retreat center in upstate New York on twenty-three acres of pasture and woodland for people from the City."

Norman has adopted unusual methods in his "interviews" with clients. He does not set an hourly fee but relies on clients to give a donation. His sessions are likely to be conducted sitting on the floor or in a restaurant or in the park. His clients regularly meet together with him as a group. His unorthodox methods develop a great deal of trust between him and his clients, which serves as the raw material for developing insight into each person's situation.

Norman was born in Brighton Beach, Brooklyn, in 1941. By the time he was fifteen he had entered New Mexico Military Institute with a view to a career as a soldier. He went on to study psychology at Ohio State University and at Aberdeen University in Scotland.

In Scotland he married Laura. They were married for sixteen years. They divorced, re-married, and then both agreed that they had started to make the same mistakes again. Rather than risk their close friendship, they divorced once more. His wife Leeny and Laura are very close friends. Norman said, "Laura is the closest family member that I have in the world. She is now my sister. The three of us meet together regularly."

Norman was one of a number of Jews who traveled to Israel at the time of the Israeli-Egyptian war in 1967. He and Laura lived in Israel from 1970 to 1973. Although from a Jewish background and a trained soldier, Norman made many friends who were Arabs or Jordanians. "Laura and I had friends on both sides. I knew I couldn't fight on either side. I didn't know how to sit in the middle of the conflicts. So at that point we left."

In New York, he began writing poetry and stories about the sea. He then spent several years living alone in the woods in New York State. It was during this period that he explored the processes of meditation. Upon his return to New York he began to receive clients. During the 1980s, he and Leeny began to receive invitations from several European countries to teach retreats and workshops. He now travels regularly to Europe with Leeny to co-teach retreats at Gaia House in Devon, and in Austria.

This interview is an exploration of his methods and of his concerns about the state of mind of people living in a goal-oriented society, where personal achievement is God.

•

CT: You work as a psychotherapist in New York. New York is intense, aggressive, stressful. What kind of clients do you work with?

NR: The words "stressful" and "aggressive" do not really describe New York. New York is desperate. It has a meanness to it that makes the people who come to me desperate for warmth, a place where they can at least be heard and, if a miracle happens, understood.

CT: What makes New York desperate?

NR: People are constantly competing with each other in a hard, cold, cut-throat way and this is accepted as a fact of life here. No matter what profession you are talking about, this is what you find, with rare exceptions. The competition for affordable living space is also fierce. And the number of enormously talented people trying their luck here is very high. No matter how good you are at what you do, here you're just one more blade of grass on the lawn. Despite your talent, you might not get a chance. That's frightening.

At a less competitive, less frenetic pace, they might function well inside the limits imposed by their problems. But in New York all of their buttons start popping off. The thing they have fallen back on all of their life—their specialness—isn't getting them the recognition and rewards they want, and a psychological explosion takes place. With so much of their energy focused on the competitiveness, they literally begin to fall apart.

CT: What kind of relationship do you develop with the client?

NR: Hopefully, an honest one. First and foremost, I want this individual to realize that the problems being brought to me do not make him or her an inferior person, a failure, someone who needs to be told what to do. Usually, new clients are emotionally exhausted. They need a place to at least regain strength and confidence. They need to feel welcome. And the first thing that happens is that they are terribly suspicious of me. Why not? They walk into a studio that has virtually no furniture, just rugs, cushions, a few small bookshelves, no pictures on the wall, nothing that resembles their idea of what psychotherapy is about. I don't wear a suit, probably haven't shaved for a few days, and my clothes look like they were picked out by my mother twenty years ago. What is more, they have come for a session that will last from one and a half to two hours and there is no fee. They will have to decide what to give me for my time and effort. Now this is so antithetical to what they are experiencing in New York, it is really unsettling. So initially, all of the suspicion is out—"Who is this guy? What's the gimmick?"

CT: Why are you working this way rather than specifying what you need from a session? What is your motive here?

NR: I have tried at various times to set a fee. There are many things I'd like to do for my wife and my former wife . . . . I've spent many nights thinking about doing it, but I simply cannot. Something inside changes when I think of charging; it becomes too much like commerce. I do a lot of work with my hands, using a form of healing touch. I don't want to feel as though I'm selling my hands to people in distress. If they are essentially free to determine what my services are worth to them and what they can afford—and this is by no means an easy balance to strike—then I don't feel as though I'm for sale. It frees me to just help them.

CT: The person faces a simplicity of setting, a certain informality in relationship, and no request for a specific fee. What kind of responses come when people get exposed to all this?

NR: Despite their suspicion and fear, despite themselves, most open up. Something says to them, "This is real." And the part of themselves that has been waiting for this responds. That starts in motion another process: the fear that what they say about themselves will make me dislike them. So they begin speaking and at the same time try to hide—or at least clean up—the details. This is where the touching and meditation work is particularly effective, in breaking down that conditioned fear of the truth.

CT: Do you have to establish trust in order to touch someone?

NR: People hear about me from their friends, coworkers, those they know and trust enough to try me out. That helps. But even so I might have to wait a while before I can touch someone very gently at the back of the neck and the crown of the head. It varies from person to person. I've been working with one individual for more than two years who still can't allow it. Being touched is incredibly difficult for many people. So I will spend a lot of time working only in relatively "safe" areas, like the back of the neck and the crown, before I invite someone to lie down and learn about deep relaxation, how to find strength and comfort in the feeling of the ground, the freedom to be therapeutically touched.

CT: What is the purpose behind touching somebody?

NR: It involves a powerful transfer and infusion of energy. Not my energy, but the natural energy around us being concentrated and directed through me into the person being touched. It is warm, reassuring, and heartfelt. People who wouldn't speak about some troubled or difficult area of their life have the support inside at that point to begin. Suddenly their mind is sharper, the process of insight opens up, and there is an ability to say aloud the hidden things that elsewhere might make you a pariah.

CT: The work of the hands allows a person to open up their heart to you. Do you find this a speedier vehicle than to just dialogue with a client?

NR: Absolutely. From a lifetime of talking, the client has built up a variety of dialogue defenses, verbal evasions. You can fence with them indefinitely, and it's unnecessary. For example, one person from another part of the country did some very wonderful work with a therapist there before beginning with me. In describing the difference between his approach and mine, she said, "You're very similar, but with you I get there faster." Here is where I value speed. Without getting hooked on results, I do want to see my clients recover from their emotional wounds as quickly as they can, and the use of touch facilitates that.

CT: What common kinds of suffering and significant changes come to mind?

NR: One of the most striking involved a woman who was convinced that she had been molested by her father. When she talked, she would insist it had happened. But whenever she was on the ground, in a deep state, being touched gently on the head, heart, abdomen, and back, the memories that returned to her were of a loving father playing with a small child; games that were affectionate but innocent. In that deep state, she loved him, delighted in his attention. This led to the discovery that her mother had interpreted their play as lewd, dirty. In ordinary conversation she superimposed her mother's viewpoint on her own, clear memories, obscuring them so much that she had cut herself off from her father. I remember the session in which it just "dropped in." She was in tears, thanking me for giving her back her father. And I was in tears, reminding her to call the therapist who had worked with her for years before me. Everybody should be in tears with this one.

But neither he nor I returned her memories to her; it was this beautiful, powerful energy that touches the heart so deeply, gives us the courage to see through our confusion. However you are comfortable naming it—as universal life force, or as God—we are describing a presence of such magnitude that it can free us from our worst fears and delusions. When I say to a client, "Time to go to the ground, time to touch," it is really an invitation to regain spirit, to feel this fully alive again.

CT: Would you say that working with their past is the primary thread of your work?

NR: Not really. In the example I just used, all the work done in relation to the woman's present circumstances wasn't mentioned. A good session is a finely tuned balance of past and present. It can't be otherwise because the past is alive in everything we are doing right now. Without being incorporated in the present moment, an investigation of the past is merely an archaeological expedition, dead fact; however fascinating, it won't change what is happening today.

CT: Let us explore other kinds of clients and their personalities. Drug addicts, prostitutes, criminals . . . what happens in these kinds of relationships? How do you deal with people living a nightmare existence?

NR: The first thing they have to feel from me is that it doesn't make a difference to me whether I'm talking to a druggie or a hooker or the president of the Chase Manhattan Bank. I am not going to react to their lives according to a rule of law that sets them apart from the so-called good people. The issue is not what they are doing but how they are going about it, whether or not they are living in harmony with their own desires and

> "I know thieves I would trust with my life—and have. I am primarily interested in the quality of a person's behavior, its essential nature, not the label it goes under."

the consequences of their actions. In that respect, it doesn't matter to me what people do. Once clients realize this, they have a much easier time talking to me, even without touch.

It is a mistake to assume that the only nightmare existences are the socially unacceptable professions. Emotionality is just as addictive as drugs; depression is just as much of a chemical substance in this sense as heroin or cocaine. I know thieves I would trust with my life—and have. I am primarily interested in the quality of a person's behavior, its essential nature, not the label it goes under. When I look at my own life, I can see my own grey areas, my own addictive behaviors, my own propensity to respond to appetite rather than reason. It is not difficult, for example, to find elements of prostitution in what I do. You come to Norm's studio and he loves you for a couple of hours and you leave some money on the way out. What does that sound like?

On Monday evenings I have a meditation class for all the people who do private sessions with me. It's beautiful to see them all sitting together, learning Vipassana [insight meditation], the touching work, becoming known to each other by how they work, not by the names they wear in society.

What they are learning in this aspect of the work is how to be themselves in front of others without shame or guilt. When I'm asked personal questions, I give as complete an answer as I can: they'll hear about the drugs, the army, all the wars, beginning with growing up in the streets of Brooklyn. One person remarked in shock, "How can you sit up there and tell such horrible stories about yourself?" Because they are true.

CT: What is the value for the client to hear about your experience? For example, psychoanalysts don't give a whisper of information about themselves. They regard themselves as being a blank sheet.

NR: That's artificial and unnatural. I never met a blank sheet I wanted to talk to. We are in this together. I have had certain experiences that have moved me to discover certain things. I'm educated in the intricacies of the mind and the possibilities of the spirit. If you filter out this training and experience, there is not a whole lot of difference between me and my clients. On my own level, I must contend with my own problems, my own fears and hesitation. If they can't sense that I mean this, then I am just one more authority in their lives that they are forced by their pain to follow. Our work ceases to be an educating conversation, a moment of guidance, instruction from someone they trust.

CT: The woman asked, "Norman, how can you tell such things about yourself?" There is evidently some surprise, if not shock, at what you say about yourself.

NR: But it is the truth. If I've done these things and learned something from them, the sense of shame about them can obviously be let go of, put to rest. But if I'm still ashamed of them, if I'm still ducking the truth about myself, then what can I possibly have to say about human behavior that would be of value to others? Human beings, even the best of us, do some outrageous things in the course of our lives. That is not something to hide.

CT: It seems there is a mutual experience of sharing and opening up going on between yourself and the client.

NR: Very much so.

CT: One of the classic problems seems to be projection upon the therapist. Does that influence or affect that relationship in any way? Your personal history could increase the sense of awe and wonder, "This guy has worked through so much." Your history could accelerate the projection.

NR: This isn't just a matter of me talking about myself. The information has to be relevant to what the client is talking about. And it can't take over the conversation; it serves as a foundation that enables the client to continue, to reach a moment of understanding. It is instructional, not confessional. For example, if someone is unable to take their next step, I'll let them know where I am hesitating, let them see how I deal with that problem. Then we have a conversation starting about the 10,000 ways to deal with being stuck.

CT: What's the difference between the two of you?

NR: After all these years, I've finally learned how to move myself through the barriers that keep arising. They still haven't discovered that; they still need a guide.

CT: Concepts like "energy" and "God" can become abstract, so one really can't relate to them. Would you say your work is primarily psychotherapy, that is, working on unresolved emotional problems? Where does "energy" or "God" fit in?

NR: My work is whatever the person in front of me needs it

to be. For some, a more verbal approach supported by the other practices is necessary; for others, we begin with more emphasis on meditation or on learning how to develop their communication with subtle energies. In all cases, the work stays rooted in specific experiences. It becomes what the person does, not an abstract.

CT: You have a number of resources available to you: hands, energy, meditation, communication.

NR: That's right. And within this range, I'll be whatever the person walking through the door needs me to be. This also changes from session to session; people seldom present only one continuous need.

CT: What happens if the person, over weeks or months, gives you the feeling that he or she is not really interested in deep fundamental change? You are a shoulder to cry on, someone to talk to who listens. What do you do in this circumstance?

NR: Call attention to it, quickly and very directly. That's easy for me. Subtlety in conversation isn't one of the things Brooklyn is famous for. I'll tell the person, "Look, I have heard this twenty times and it's getting boring. You might be able to do this for the next three years, but I'm not interested in that. Either you start moving or I stop listening."

CT: What kind of response do you get?

NR: Most of the time, the person snaps out of it once the shock of being invited to leave wears off. Even if people don't have much experience with directness, they do seem to appreciate it. Once I was with a client who insisted on returning to old issues long resolved as a way of keeping the conversation safe. She was paying zero attention to what I was saying, so finally I warned her that if she kept it up, I'd rather watch television. She ignored that too, so I turned on the set, watched a movie for about fifteen minutes. Then I asked her if she had had enough of this. She had. Seeing me turn away from her had sobered her up. We went back to work and she really began to talk. On another occasion, when I was working seventy to seventy-five hours a week, I told a client, "Give me some help here. Make it interesting or you are going to lose me." She looked at me and saw that I really was fading out. That woman did the best session she had done in months.

CT: The "idle rich" come to see you because it is almost fashionable. Do the yuppies come to see you who simply want to feel comfortable with their lifestyle—their consumerism and obsession with making money?

NR: People who don't want to work, rich or poor, don't stay very long. I won't let them spin the litanies about themselves indefinitely, and the meditation process also makes it difficult for them to indulge themselves. Stillness is a means for

> "Being open does not mean only experiencing pleasantness; it involves a willingness to deal with whatever life offers at the moment. New York is a marvelous classroom for teaching that."

insight. Just experiencing the flow of the breath or the feeling of the ground creates room for impulses to surface that the person has been working very hard to bury beneath the consumerism. When that happens, the client either decides to face the issues or quits.

CT: A common conception of New York is that it is an environment of tension and hostility. Through touch, communication, meditation, their inner world is revealed through the release of emotional material. You are with this person for a two-hour period. Then they are back on the streets of New York, possibly quite vulnerable. Their defenses and resistances have dropped away. How does the person make the transition from an intense session with you back to being in Manhattan?

NR: With difficulty, but it is a part of the process. Being open does not mean only experiencing pleasantness; it involves a willingness to deal with whatever life offers at the moment. New York is a marvelous classroom for teaching that. If I see that somebody is too vulnerable, I might let them rest in the apartment and take my next client for a walk. I do a lot of sessions outdoors, by the river or in Central Park. It doesn't inhibit the touching work, either. In this city, nobody is alarmed by the sight of someone's head and neck being touched. I could be standing on the person's chest; as long as we weren't blocking traffic, no one would care.

CT: Isn't there the possibility of clients going through anxiety waiting to see you again the following week?

NR: Yes, but they know that they can always call me if things get difficult. I'll spend time on the phone with them; this softens the sense of separation.

CT: Isn't there the possibility that out of insight and appreciation clients will become dependent upon you? What is the process for completing their work with you?

NR: In the beginning, of course they become dependent. Their safety lies in the fact that I don't want them to remain tied to me by an inability to work on their own. This is not just a clinical situation, a place to fix broken personalities. It is an educational process, a matter of learning how to see into the process of life itself. I'll assign novels and poems where they highlight something a client needs to learn, do sessions in restaurants or in swimming pools—whatever is needed to get the point across and help the person integrate what we do and discuss into his or her daily life. This is where the meditation work and the subtle energy exercises are particularly valuable. You have to do them on you own. I can't sit and breathe for you.

CT: In the total process of the interaction between you and the client, signals come clear to you that the person is taking responsibility for their life.

NR: The shift is most noticeable in relation to everyday decisions that the client has to make. Instead of wanting me to make the decision, the person becomes more vocal, using me as a sounding board for his or her own ideas, or maybe even telling me about decisions already made. At that point, the person is no longer being overwhelmed by problems. That's when the conversation really gets interesting. There are reasons then to continue working with me. They may develop a love of meditation and energy work and decide to study it more deeply as a subject independent of their problems. They may be ready to step beyond the body into other realms of existence. But now they are not *compelled* to stay with me; I become a real choice.

CT: How do you respond to clients whose lifestyle really contributes to their unhappiness?

NR: By making that the subject of our work right from the beginning. Recently, a young man from New York came to Devon to work with me on that very problem. At home he was working a seventy-hour week at a job he no longer enjoyed. Merely knowing the reasons why he was burying himself this way wasn't changing anything, and after every session I would point this out to him, that nothing would be different until he made room in his schedule for it to be so—until he put down the drug, stopped overdosing on work. On retreat here, he began learning how to do that.

CT: Having made changes in their relationship to their activities, so there is balance and integration, what is the meditation going to do for them?

NR: Insight meditation enables them to see beyond their immediate circumstances into the very nature of themselves, the heart and soul of the unknown. They can begin examining more clearly their relationship to neighbors, community, nation, and beyond this to the universe and the unknown, which we approach through the reality of death.

CT: What you are describing is a movement for the client from a state of personal suffering and desperation to its transformation in the transcendent issues of life beyond personal circumstances.

NR: Yes, it's the blending of these two aspects of existence that enables us to complete our development as human beings. I know there is a lot of conversation about the difference between meditation and psychotherapy, but I have always looked upon them as complementary processes. You must deal with the issue of self in relation to the universe in which the self has been formed. Which aspect you begin with depends upon which tools you favor. I like the personal approach. I love working directly with people, being in the mud with them, and in the process helping them find the peace within that enables them to journey into the larger context.

CT: Even in New York?

NR: Especially in New York!

The Sensitized Mind

An interview with Roger Walsh

Roger Walsh is a professor in the department of Psychiatry and Human Behavior at the University of California in Irvine. In 1981, he spent several months in Burma and Thailand, ostensibly to practice meditation. What he saw and experienced there "shook the foundations" of his life.

The result of his trip was *Staying Alive: The Psychology of Human Survival,* nominated by *New Options* as one of the best political books of 1985. It deals with the state of the mind, the state of the world, and the healing of the planet. In it he writes:

> Standing on a street corner [in Burma] for an hour, I learned as much about diseases and leprosy, congenital deformities and tuberculosis of the spine as I had learned in medical school.
>
> The amount of preventable suffering was staggering. Overpopulation, poverty, malnutrition, pollution, disease; all were wreaking an extraordinary and unnecessary amount of pain.
>
> How could I have been so asleep? How could I have repressed the extent of preventable pain?

Returning to California, he experienced a profound culture shock and found an answer to his questions. Most activities in his Western world "seemed to aim at a continuous distraction away from deeper, more important concerns."

Roger has told me that for years his experiences with meditation were characterized by pain and difficulty, yet they persistently challenged his basic beliefs and assumptions about himself. Being challenged in this way made the pain of the process workable. More recently, he has found access to spiritual joy during deep mediation. Roger regularly flies from his West Coast home to attend meditation retreats at the Insight Meditation Society in Barre, Massachussetts. His inner exploration directly influences his professional work because, as he points out, the problems are both "out there" and "in here."

Roger is coeditor of *Beyond Ego* and *Beyond Health and Normality* and has written numerous articles for the *American Journal of Psychiatry* and the *Journal of Humanistic Psychology*. His most recent book is *The Spirit of Shamanism*. He is married to Frances Vaughan, a professor at the California Institute of Transpersonal Psychology. Our interview took place in Santa Rosa, California, on a break during a ten-day retreat.

•

CT: In your book *Staying Alive*, you refer to the problems of the planet as having their roots in psychological factors, including greed, aggression, and ignorance. This implies the necessity to look both inwardly and outwardly at ourselves and the world. What part does religion have to play in facing the planet?

RW: I think it can play a crucial part because we are at a new phase in human history. For the first time, our technological power and our capacity to change the world are so great that the state of the world mirrors the state of our individual and collective minds. We look out at the world and what we see are the psychological forces and conflicts within us and between us mirrored back to us. What we see, therefore, are our *own* psychological and spiritual conflicts, distortions, and deficiencies reflected as the world's problems of our time.

Now, classically, religions have, at least in their higher or mystical forms, provided us with pathways for training the mind to reduce intra- and interpersonal conflict. Through these methods, the emotions which create conflict, such as hatred and greed, are transformed into more socially beneficial emotions and behaviors such as love, compassion, and joy for another's well-being. Psychology also aims at helping us to reduce negative qualities and cultivate the positive in the mind. At this time in history, religion and psychology may have increasingly more important roles to play, not only in individual well-being but also in our social and collective well-being.

CT: Sometimes the association with religion is nothing much more than ritual, a strong belief system, and possibly fundamentalism, which some people feel is distant from global reality.

RW: That is a very important point and, indeed, I'm using the term in a very specific way, which I should explain. I'm not referring so much to the popular rituals and beliefs which are so often mistaken for the totality of religious possibility, and I'm certainly not referring to the rigid dogmas which have been the source of so much conflict and suffering. Rather, I'm pointing to something which is only now starting to become well known, and that is the common core of contemplative practices and wisdom found at the heart of all the great religions. This common core is sometimes known as the "perennial wisdom" or "perennial philosophy." What is notable about the perennial wisdom is that it emphasizes the importance of contemplative practices to train and change the mind. For centuries diverse religions have claimed that these practices—for example, meditation, yoga, and contemplation—are capable of accelerating personal and spiritual development. The interesting thing is that recent psychological research is beginning to support these claims. People who practice such disciplines tend to be both psychologically and physically healthier, and tend to live lives of less consumption and of greater voluntary simplicity; they are probably more socially concerned, and even seem to live longer.

I suspect that if these practices become more widespread they may help us live more sensitively and respond more appropriately to our current global problems. On the other hand, there's the very real danger that religious fanaticism may prevail and exacerbate our problems. Throughout human history countless millions of people have died because of their belief that "mine is the only true way." But with the kinds of weapons now at our disposal, such beliefs may be suicidal, perhaps even omnicidal. How religions are understood and practiced may help determine the fate of our species.

CT: A person may say that these various spiritual disciplines and practices are a life-long task. Meanwhile, the planet is facing global extinction.

RW: That is a classic dilemma. The question is, to what extent should we work on ourselves and to what extent should we direct our efforts to other people and the outer world? It is interesting that we tend to think of this question in extremes—that we must do one or the other. Yet, in point of fact, if one looks at history, one finds an interesting phenomenon which the great historian Arnold Toynbee called "the cycle of withdrawal and return." What he found was that those people who had contributed most to human development and well-being throughout history exhibited a common life pattern. First, they withdrew from society for a while to go inward to confront their questions and fears and to wrestle with the basic questions of human existence. Having come to some understanding, they then returned with that wisdom to share it with other people, having become, in the process, more effective instruments of service. Often they exhibited this cycle of withdrawal and return several times during the course of their lives.

So it is important to see that one does not need to do only one or the other, but to see that one may cycle through these two phases of inner and outer work. Of course, it is also possible to combine them so that one goes out into the world not only to heal and serve, but also to learn and awaken oneself and others in the process. Going out into the world then leads one deeper into oneself. In the East this has been known as "karma yoga," the yoga of service and work in the world. In the West, it has been known as service and learning. There doesn't have to be the sharp distinction between serving others and enhancing one's own well-being. The two may eventually merge.

CT: In the West, would you say that a contemporary example of "withdrawal and return" would be people going into retreats or workshops for renewal and then going back into daily life?

RW: Yes, certainly. And I think we are seeing greater numbers of people doing that and seeing more products of that. In fact, my book, *Staying Alive*, was a result of this process. There is no way that I could have written the book without the inspiration that retreats gave me.

CT: What kind of influence, if any, is this having on our major institutions—the established churches, politics, medicine, science, education?

> "Especially in mature and psychologically healthy people, the upper levels of psychological development seem to look suspiciously like the early stages of spiritual development."

RW: My own feeling is that some inroads are being made but that they are still quite small. In the last decade, traditional churches have shown a dramatic resurgence of interest in contemplation. In education, there are clearly some effects, though again small. There is an increasing number of courses being given in religious studies and on the psychology of the contemplative traditions. There is a whole new area of psychology called "transpersonal psychology," which studies those states of consciousness in which there is an experience of the sense of self expanding beyond (trans) the usual personality or ego limits. Some of these transpersonal states have been regarded historically as the *summum bonum* or highest goal of human existence by several religions.

This attempt by psychologists to understand what were once thought of as purely religious phenomena is beginning to expand our understanding of human development. To give an example of the impact that it is having: within the last decade, Western psychologists have dramatically increased their exploration of adult development. Especially in mature and psychologically healthy people, the upper levels of psychological development seem to look suspiciously like the early stages of spiritual development. In the last few years, we have begun to see the first full spectrum models of development which trace human psychological development from infancy through normal adulthood and then beyond, into various spiritual stages and even into levels of enlightenment.

CT: How would you describe the difference between a psychologically healthy human being and one who is living with spiritual insights and awareness?

RW: First, we have to appreciate that there is considerable overlap. A psychologically healthy person is one who experiences a minimum of conflict and defensiveness. There is considerable data to show that this type of person is one who tends to be altruistic and generous, and derives that satisfaction from the process of giving of themselves. It is interesting to look at that and see that these are characteristics that are classically descriptive of religious development and maturity. A person who has a degree of spiritual insight and understanding might have access to a range of altered states of consciousness. He or she might have a deeper understanding of their self-nature, or transpersonal nature, that is beyond the personality or the ego. That person might identify primarily with consciousness rather than with the body. He or she might sometimes experience a unitive state of consciousness in which there is compassion for all beings, not just one's friends or family, but all living beings. In such a state of mind, the sense of identity becomes increasingly encompassing, with fewer dichotomies or distinction from other people.

CT: Both a psychologically healthy person and a spiritually conscious person often seem to show a definite resistance to being engaged in the troubles of the world.

RW: I think that can certainly happen, but I wonder if this resistance hasn't been exaggerated in many cases. We hear so often that people who are concerned with self-actualization, self-growth, self-exploration, etc., are nothing but narcissistic and selfish. Now I'm sure that this *can* be the case, but I'm not sure it's always or even often the case. In fact, research shows clearly that psychologically healthy and mature people tend to be more altruistic and socially concerned than other people. But, as you say, some individuals involved in psychological and spiritual growth work may not be particularly involved in immediate social or political contribution. But again, I don't think that we should rush to judge them. Some of them may indeed have become overly withdrawn from social involvement. On the other hand, for some of them it may be only a temporary phase before they find themselves drawn to share whatever they've learned. Another positive interpretation is that some people feel that their greatest contributions may come from changing and healing minds, including their own, rather than working on specific projects or things in the world.

That viewpoint gains increasing credence if we recognize, as I think we are forced to, that the state of the world today really does reflect our state of mind. Also, there seems to be a developmental process that people in spiritual practice go through. First, they become increasingly sensitized to their experience, both inner and outer. Then they find themselves less and less able to keep out the pain and suffering of the world and more and more sensitive to the cries for help that pour forth from every television screen and every quarter of the globe. An enormous, indeed incomprehensible, amount of suffering surrounds us. Someone with a sensitized mind is increasingly pulled to work to alleviate this suffering in whatever ways that he or she can. I find that as I go around and speak to people about the state of the world what gives me hope is the growing number of people who are committing their lives to working with global issues. I find that very inspiring.

CT: What is your response when a person says, "Well, what can I do except work on myself?"

RW: I think the first thing to realize is that this is not a simple question. Most of us, when we first awaken to the crises and suffering in the world, do so with an enormous sense of urgency. We think we should know immediately what is the best contribution we can make. We often fail to realize that this question is really one of the most profound and complex that we as individuals and humankind have ever faced. It may be very important to be patient and, at least for a while, be willing not to know what to do. In fact, not knowing may be part of the answer. If we look around the world we find that a lot of the world's problems are caused by people who think that they know what the answers are and then impose their answers on others.

CT: The first step, then, is not knowing and retaining the question.

RW: Exactly. We need to realize that the question, "How can I best contribute to healing our global crisis?" is not something we answer overnight. For me, it took almost two years from the time of recognizing how urgent the world situation is until I could see that I might be able to contribute through working on the psychology of human survival. Taking time can be very important. Let it be okay not to know. We really crucify ourselves with "the tyranny of shoulds." We have the idea that we should be able to come up with answers immediately. Precipitous action may not be helpful. Reflective action is much more likely to be strategic.

The second thing which I think is important for us to do is to take some time to educate ourselves. This education has to be of two types. First, it has to be about the state of the world and the problems we are facing so we can act with awareness and respond in a strategic way. The second type of education we need is about the psychological and spiritual causes which have created the problems in the first place, so that we can act with understanding. The famous English author H.G. Wells said, "History becomes increasingly a race between education and catastrophe." So education of both ourselves and others is crucial.

The third step is not only to look at the question of what I can do but what I truly *want* to do. We are most likely to be effective if the work we are doing is a path of the heart and consistent with our deeper wishes. True contribution doesn't have to be a sacrifice. Most of us have the idea that it is. That can be a very self-destructive idea.

CT: Why is that?

RW: Firstly, it leads to burnout because we are acting out of "shoulds" instead of "wants." Secondly, it leads to resentment and anger which, of course, takes the joy out of the whole process. Yet what we are trying to do is to increase joy and reduce suffering. It's not likely to be helpful if we work in ways which create more suffering.

The fourth step in social-global contribution is to look for groups of like-minded people. There is strength in numbers. One of the things which I find most encouraging is the increase in the number of globally oriented groups in the last few years. I recently looked up *The Encyclopedia of Organizations* in the United States and found that half the globally concerned groups here had been formed within the last five years. I find that very encouraging.

CT: Are there other considerations for action?

RW: The fifth thing, I think, is to play a kind of game with ourselves. It is not only to ask what I can do but what is the most strategic thing I can do. We can look at optimizing our impact, using the inspirational examples of people like Mother

Teresa or Gandhi. We tend to think of these people as spiritual geniuses who could automatically come up with marvelous ideas and solutions. But if we look carefully at their lives, we find they often spent long periods in contemplation, prayer, and reflection, seeking inspiration as to what would be the most strategic contributions that they could make. The game we could play might be: "If Mother Teresa or Mahatma Gandhi were living *my* life, with my friends, skills, and connections, what would they do?"

CT: Some people tell me there are so many issues they don't know what to turn to. It seems our society takes up hot-off-the-press issues like child abuse, drugs, South Africa, famine, Nicaragua, AIDS, nuclear weapons, the forests. There is a tremendous burst of public interest and then the issue is forgotten because a new issue, a new crisis, has arisen. How does one sustain commitment in spite of the hype which goes up and down in waves of newsprint?

RW: It sounds like you are asking two questions. One is how to choose an issue, and second, how to maintain dedication to it. Ultimately, we can only trust our own sense of what seems right for us to do, because there are no hard and fast rules that speak to our unique situation. Only we can know when it is appropriate to stay with an issue and when it is appropriate to change. However, perhaps one can work across a wide range of problems by appreciating that the fundamental causes of our collective problems are not purely military, economic, and political, but also psychological and spiritual. To the extent that one is working on these deeper dimensions, both within oneself and the world, one is working not only on the so-called problems—which are actually symptoms—but also the underlying causes.

CT: This is why the interfacing of ourselves and totality becomes so important, because our heart and minds are connected to the world.

RW: There's considerable data emerging from psychology showing that service contributes to psychological and, presumably, also spiritual well-being, as the sages have claimed across history. I think there may be a fundamental error in the assumption that we have to be completely integrated and enlightened before we can serve.

CT: You live and work in California. A growing number of people here use the invaluable resources of psychotherapy and meditation. But in many places in the West people think, "I'm not neurotic. I don't need a therapist."

RW: I think you are right. In much of the world, psychotherapy is only used for the seriously disturbed. As yet there is little appreciation that therapy and meditation can enhance well-being in normal people and also make them more willing and able to be helpful to others and be socially involved.

> "What is little known in our culture is that when the desire for truth, realization, and transcendence is not acknowledged within oneself, it results in types of pathology —like cynicism, alienation, meaninglessness, or addiction."

CT: Doesn't consumerism hinder human beings from being in touch with important social and existential questions?

RW: I think it more than hinders. I think it is actually a defense mechanism against the recognition of these issues. Consumerism and the insatiable demand for ever more stimulation and gratification through money, power, drugs, sex, food, and possessions can actually be substitute gratifications for higher needs. What is little known in our culture is that when the desire for truth, realization, and transcendence is not acknowledged within oneself, it results in types of pathology—like cynicism, alienation, meaninglessness, or addiction. Not knowing that this is an existential pathology and not knowing how to deal with it, the mind turns to the old gratifications. But since these gratifications are not what we really need, and since we can never get enough of what we don't really need, we end up in a vicious cycle of compulsively consuming more and more, yet feeling fundamentally unsatisfied.

What is also not acknowledged is that the addiction to consumption is actually just that—an addiction. One then needs increasing amounts for one's fix—whether the fix be possessions, power, status, or sex—in order to get the same results.

CT: There is some public awareness about the addiction to alcohol and drugs, but little about consumerism.

RW: One of the important things that Asian wisdom traditions have to teach us is that we can become addicted to anything, internal or external. Society has not yet appreciated that, and we and our planet are suffering greatly because of it.

Prescription for Action

Roger Walsh

1. Realize that the question "How can I best contribute to healing our global crisis?" is not something you will answer overnight.

2. Take some time to educate yourself about both the state of the world and the psychological and spiritual causes that have created the problems.

3. Ask yourself: What do I truly *want* to do? Find a path consistent with your deeper wishes.

4. Look for groups of like-minded people. There is strength and encouragement in numbers.

5. Ask yourself: If Mother Teresa or Mahatma Gandhi were living *my* life, with my friends, skills, and connections, what would she or he do? Spend time in reflection in order to discover the most strategic contribution you can make.

ORDER FORM

10% DISCOUNT on orders of $20 or more —
20% DISCOUNT on orders of $50 or more —
30% DISCOUNT on orders of $250 or more —
On cost of books for fully prepaid orders

NAME

ADDRESS

CITY   STATE   ZIP

COUNTRY (outside USA)   POSTAL CODE

TITLE	QTY	PRICE	TOTAL
The Amnesty International Handbook	@	$14.95	
The Amnesty International Report (hard)	@	$25.00	
The Amnesty International Report (soft)	@	$15.00	
Bitter Fruit (soft cover)	@	$12.95	
Bitter Fruit (hard cover)	@	$21.95	
Everyday Racism (soft cover)	@	$12.95	
Everyday Racism (hard cover)	@	$19.95	
Helping Teens Stop Violence (soft cover)	@	$11.95	
Helping Teens Stop Violence (spiral)	@	$14.95	
Human Rights for Children (soft cover)	@	$10.95	
Human Rights for Children (spiral bound)	@	$12.95	
Spirit of Change	@	$ 9.95	

Shipping costs:
*First book: $2.00
($3.00 for Canada)
Each additional book:
$.50 ($1.00 for
Canada)
For UPS rates and
bulk orders call us
at (510) 865-5282*

TOTAL
Less discount @_____% (   )
TOTAL COST OF BOOKS _____
Calif. residents add sales tax _____
Shipping & handling _____
TOTAL ENCLOSED _____
Please pay in U.S. funds only

❏ Check   ❏ Money Order   ❏ Visa   ❏ M/C

Card # _____ Exp date _____

Signature _____

Complete and mail to:
Hunter House Inc., Publishers
PO Box 2914, Alameda CA 94501-2914
Phone (510) 865-5282 Fax (510) 865-4295
❏ Check here to receive our book catalog